It Can Happen to You

50 Serendipitous, Unexpected, Out of the Blue, Life Changing Love Stories

Nancy Ripp White

The Three Tomatoes Book Publishing

Published January 2022
ISBN: 978-1-7376177-6-1
Library of Congress Control Number: 9781737617761

For information address:
The Three Tomatoes Book Publishing
6 Soundview Rd.
Glen Cove, NY 11542

Cover design: Susan Herbst
Cover photograph: Dreamstime © Viktor Bondariev
Interior design: Susan Herbst

" The thing about love was that it caught you unaware, turned up in the most unexpected places even when you weren't looking for it. "

~Sarra Manning

DEDICATION

To my 17-year-old grand-twins, Justin and Ethan.

If I can go from playing monopoly to writing this book, it proves that anything is possible...at any age!

If it can happen for me, it can happen for you.

No one is you and that is your superpower. Couple that with passion and commitment and you have the winning formula.

From my heart to yours...I love you guys,

Your YAYA

PREFACE

THERE ARE 86,400 SECONDS IN every day and each one is precious.

How many of those seconds do you spend thinking, hoping, and dreaming about when and if your love partner is going to show up? We often spend these seconds strategizing on how to make romance happen or spend our seconds on self-defeating inner thoughts. The strategies are endless. The dating sites, swiping right or left, encouraging good friends to set you up, smiling at the handsome guy at the dog park... most, to no avail.

I've been fascinated and curious about relationships since I was a young teen. My fascination kept growing until I realized this was it. I wanted love to be my full-time career. I wanted to focus on all matters of the heart and so I became a certified life coach, specializing in relationships.

My degree in coaching did not include a magic wand that could take away all the negative thoughts that might be keeping my clients from having the love they want. I don't have a wand, but what I do have to offer are fifty stories of magical love connections to share with you.

All of these stories happened because they were meant to be.

You will be surprised, delighted, and hopeful when reading them. My hope is they will encourage you to be open to the unexpected.

Settle into a cozy chair with a cup of tea or a glass of wine. Pull up your favorite playlist and enjoy reading about people just like you.

The stories range from falling in love with your surgeon after having brain surgery, to finding the love of your life on the baseball field.

Taking on a career in love requires a lot of research. Some clinical, some up close. I ask almost everyone I meet how they found love. And the most intriguing element was the diversity: What made them tick? What goes into a successful relationship, or what was missing in the mismatch that seemed so perfect on paper?

After years of coaching women, of all ages, after the obvious personal growth, I finally realized that so much of finding a love partner had to do with the unexpected. The serendipitous, out-of-the-blue encounters that changed lives in the blink of an eye.

I decided to gather these unexpected, serendipitous, out-of-the-ordinary, atypical stories, knowing that everyone adores a good love story, and to give women of all ages inspiration, hope, and possibilities. Confirming that it is never too late to discover and say yes to love.

Each story is personal and unique. How you fall in love at thirty is very different than how you fall in love at sixty. But there is a common thread throughout the stories. All the participants woke up in the morning without a love partner and by the end of the day, something amazing occurred that they never expected, and love grew out of that unexpected event.

So, ladies, this book is dedicated to all of you. You, who thought love forgot your address. You, who thought, *Well, he's not rich enough, tall enough, young enough.* You, who thought, *Why bother?*

Fate knows your address and it knows that love will find you in the most serendipitous way. Read all the stories. You'll laugh, you'll cry, you'll see yourself on the pages. And you'll be convinced that love is truly meant to be.

Remember, the word *hopeless* begins with hope. Spend your seconds wisely. Put them to good use. Both fate and love know where you live. And they will find you!

TABLE OF CONTENTS

66 Love is uncontrollable. You do
not know when it will come and
how it will happen. 99

~Unknown

QUARANTINE LOVE
Allison & Eric

1

I REALLY LOVED DATING. YES, I really did. I found out so much about myself and learned a great deal about men in general.

The men and dates I went on ranged from the sublime to the ridiculous.

I had wonderful romantic dates, and those where I was counting the minutes until I could make my escape, but it was all good.

I had my share of disappointments but also had wonderful nights to always remember.

I had postponed getting into a serious relationship because I just wasn't ready to settle down.

It was actually fun because there wasn't any pressure put on myself or the men I was dating.

However, I only wanted to be married once and wanted to make sure I was really ready.

At thirty-two, just when I felt ready, COVID struck. We were all quarantined!

Personal growth was important to me and so I kept myself open to any life lessons that were available. I read self-help books. I Zoomed in on many seminars. I podcasted, and I watched more than my share of TV. Thank you, Netflix.

I remember waking up earlier in the week, thinking about my life and how the heck was I going to meet anyone being in my house 24/7. We were all working from home, not even going to the grocery store!

Did I make a mistake? Did I wait too long? For the first time I was doubting my life choices.

Most of my friends were married and had someone to be with during these crazy times. I envied them. I was feeling very lonely and a little scared.

I kept busy. I'm an art director so it was easy to make the transition to working remotely during the day, but the nights were very long. Very!

On that fateful night, it was close to midnight. My apartment building in New York City was quiet when I snuck out into the hallway in my sweats, to throw out my garbage.

A tall knight appeared, not in shiny armor but also in sweats coming out of the elevator with an adorable dog. One I had never seen before...the man, nor the dog.

He startled me, pleasantly. Although we were both masked, I could tell that he was a nice-looking man. Where did he come from? I thought that I knew everyone on my floor.

We introduced ourselves and I quickly found out that he had come to visit his cousin before the epidemic and couldn't fly back to his home in California.

Masked, we spoke for over an hour, both starved for company. After about fifteen minutes we moved to the floor to continue our conversation, feeling both comfortable and intrigued with one another. I likened it to meeting a stranger at a masked ball. Exciting!

We decided to meet the same way the next night (a little earlier) and the next and the next.

This was an amazing way to meet a special person. We had so much to discuss. He too is a personal growth student, which made for deep conversations. It was easy and comfortable.

Soon after, we both got tested for COVID and finally were able to unmask. We were both pleasantly surprised!

We moved our visits to my place and have been together ever since.

On the first anniversary of our first meeting, we re-created the scene in the hallway in our sweats and of course with his dog. And to my surprise, he proposed.

If I could meet someone during a pandemic, then anything is possible!

Keep believing in yourself and the universe to bring you love when it's time.

As the saying goes, "Don't quit before the miracle!"

2

Day 180
Kate & Arthur

Day 180. Two more days makes six months without a date, without anyone asking for my phone number, without the valet attendant even giving me a second glance!

Why not me? I'm looking pretty darn good for forty-one. I have a fabulous job where, by the way, I meet a lot of men—mad men in advertising. What more could a girl want? A date, perhaps. It's not happening.

Tonight, I'm driving to a business dinner with a highly successful automotive account executive at a top agency. This is a woman who lives in a man's world of cars, creative, and big budgets. Yes, she is a bit intimidating, so I am driving around the block making mental notes of what to talk to her about! Dinner could go either way—fun or failure.

We women like to talk about the men in our lives—or the lack thereof. This executive is engaged and tells me all about the plans for the house they are building. I'm thinking she must know a lot of his men friends and men at work. I'll share my game plan with her.

Game Plan. Tell friends, family, and strangers that I would like to be in a relationship, and I am open to meeting someone. Easier said than done.

Dinner starts out a little awkward since we don't really know each other that well. But, as soon as I start telling her about my dating dilemma, the ice breaks and we are two chicks talking men.

She immediately tells me about this single, divorced, fabulous friend of her fiancé. She'll arrange everything. We chat about him for a while. Then she declares that she is the matchmaking queen and right now she is ten to zero on matches that have led to marriage. She asks if I am serious about this game plan of mine, because she wants to maintain her winning streak!

Well, the dinner was a home run. Her winning streak held and here we are thirty-plus years later. My husband and I live in South America and are very much in love and happy. The matchmaker became a good friend and was honored that her winning streak was upheld and that she was mentioned in our wedding vows.

You never know how love is going to find you. Be sure to tell everyone you know that you are available!

He Said No
Pamela & Neil

3

I FIRST HEARD OF NEIL, NEWLY divorced, from my Aunt Ronnie who was referred to him by my cousin who hired Neil, a Realtor, to find him a new condo.

Aunt Ronnie and I always had similar tastes in men, and she had an immediate attraction to Neil. But he was younger, so she thought about him for her niece (me).

At the time, I was forty-two and a divorced single mom with three children. A six-, ten-, and thirteen-year-old.

Neil liked my appearance when he saw my photo, but as soon as he heard I had three young children, he decided not to call me (he has one son). I was disappointed.

A month later, I was driving home from a trip visiting my girlfriend for a beach vacation with our combined six kids in upstate Florida.

On the way home, it was pouring rain on the turnpike, and I was feeling a bit lonely. I had two tickets to the Madonna concert that Friday night and I decided to call Neil and invite him. Who said only males can invite females out?

He answered the call, said he didn't like Madonna, and said no thank you to the concert. It was a brief call and we hung up. I was furious! I called Aunt Ronnie and told her to never set me up again, as she seems to attract jerks.

The next morning at work, my phone rang. It was Neil.

He said he could hardly make out who he was talking to the night before as he was shopping in Publix. He admitted he didn't like Madonna, but he said he would love to take me out to dinner Saturday night. I decided to give him a chance.

After our first date, neither of us saw anyone else again and we've been together since then and have been very happily married for fifteen years. Our children feel like true siblings to each other and are all close. So, it is a very happy ending.

Never ever give up. Love happens when you least expect it.

Red Glasses
Jill & Dennis

I WAS DESPERATE, SCARED, ALONE and addicted!

I went to my first twelve-step meeting in Queens, New York and was terrified. A late-comer walked in, a guy with fabulous red glasses. I was so afraid to be in meetings but so intrigued with the guy with those glasses that I kept coming back. He always popped in late and always left early. Then after a few weeks, I stopped going to that meeting and decided to attend meetings in my hometown, far away from the other.

I was longing to be in a relationship. I hadn't dated for a year as per the twelve-step suggestions at that time. Lonely and shy, I ventured into New York City to find a meeting I had never been to, hoping to meet new people and maybe a cute guy.

Lo and behold there was the guy in red glasses. We didn't speak.

The following week I decided to attend yet another new meeting I had never been to, and yes, you guessed it, there was the guy in the red glasses!

Then one afternoon, I took my little daughter to an afternoon meeting, another location I had never gone to. And yes, there he was, red glasses and all.

This time we spoke after the meeting, my daughter by my side. I found out then that he also had never attended the three meeting locations where we spotted each other before. It was serendipity. He also told me that the reason he kept coming to the first meeting was because of the girl sitting in the back—me!

Following the program's suggestions and out of respect for me, he didn't approach me then because I was vulnerable and needed to get the program.

While talking after the meeting that afternoon my daughter, who only came up to his thighs, and was by no means a precocious kid, pulled on his pants, looking up at him with her big brown eyes, and asked if he was going to marry her mother.

I think he shuddered. He was not looking for love and marriage.

Despite her remark, he asked me to lunch anyway, and the rest is history. We dated, never saw anyone else again, and after two years of dating we were married. It's now been forty-four years! Oh, by the way, he adopted my daughter, now his daughter, and we have two granddaughters.

I've often wondered if I hadn't been working the program while learning to love myself, would my soul mate have found his way to my door in that most serendipitous way?

"There is never a time or place for true love. It happens accidentally in a heartbeat, in a single flashing, throbbing moment."

~*Unknown*

THREW IN THE TOWEL
Laura & Miquel

I SO WANTED TO MEET my soul mate and have a child. At forty-six, it seemed that part of life had passed me by.

I was feeling hopeless as I watched and witnessed my friends, one by one, meet and marry their person and wondered, Why not me?

I decided to give my life over to giving service and became an interfaith minister. I signed up to teach classes. I got excited about my life again by creating a seminar to teach meditation and teamwork.

One day a gentleman came to one of my classes. He was most definitely not my type, not my pictures. He was another race and religion but oh so smart and curious. We had wonderful deep conversations that were very stimulating, and he was very involved.

I saw him at other events, but we didn't speak. About nine months later, there was a holiday party that we both attended. He told me that he remembered me. For some reason he looked far more attractive than I had remembered.

He then said words that had shock value. "The last time I saw you, I told my roommate that I was going to marry you."

Can that be? Did he know something that I couldn't possibly know?

We continued getting to know one another and were

drawn together on a very deep level. We married when I was forty-eight and we joyfully adopted our daughter when I was fifty-three.

At seventy-four, reflecting on my life, I can knowingly say that it truly is never too late. Never stop believing. I spent way too much time in my head telling myself all the reasons why it wasn't going to happen for me, rather than focusing on what was possible.

Say yes to life and allow yourself to have feelings regarding the ones that got away or just weren't supposed to be, but not too much time!

Trust the universe. Stay in the present and please don't quit before the miracle.

6

BEST FRIENDS

Barbara & Steve

MY BROTHER'S BEST FRIEND STEPHEN lived next door to us for as long as I can remember.

Steve spent every holiday with us. Sometimes he brought a date and sometimes he came solo. He was considered a ladies' man and had no interest in getting married. For sure.

I liked him as a friend, that was all. I made him laugh and he liked that so when he asked me out and I said no, he got hurt and wouldn't speak to me for six years.

During this time, I had gotten married and had a son. I was going through a hard time while dealing with the divorce. I was sad and lonely with a small son. I no longer fit in with my married or single friends since I had a child and they didn't. I felt at thirty-seven that part of my life was going to be put on hold until my son was older and more independent.

I turned to Steve, and he rose to the occasion as a great friend. Every night we watched *Seinfeld* together by telephone. He in his apartment and me in mine!

He took my young son and me to brunch almost every week and they were very comfortable together.

Things started to shift when a friend from Los Angeles came to visit. When she showed interest in Steve, I noticed I felt uneasy. Was it jealousy, was it love? Or was it unrequited love? He wasn't interested in my friend, but I still was left unsettled with butterflies in my stomach.

He confessed his love and took my son and me to dinner. The way he treated my son sealed the deal.

You know the rest. I was not thinking of marriage, and he was a confirmed bachelor!

We have been married for twenty years and also have a daughter together. Marrying your best friend is a gift on so many levels.

You are friends first and then lovers.

Do not settle. Where there's life, there is hope! Remember, you only need one!

Defeated and Broken
Ellie & Gary

After two long-term failed relationships over the years, I was done, finished. And then I found myself deeply in love.

We were together for six years. I wanted to move forward and take what I thought was the next relationship step. He held back. Afraid of commitment. I'd be a rich woman if I had a dime for every man who used that logic.

I decided to take bold action, saying, "If you don't want to move our relationship forward, I'm moving on." And I did!

I moved to California for several months, praying that he would realize his mistake in letting me go. It worked. Or so I thought.

After five months he called to say "I can't live like this anymore. I love you. Come home. We'll get engaged."

I was overjoyed. I immediately disassembled my California apartment, sold my car, and returned home.

Two weeks later he admitted that he had made a terrible mistake. I was heartbroken, really heartbroken.

I totally swore off men, and for the next three years I didn't go out socially except for weekend lunches with girl-friends. That's right. No men, no dates, just day and night work.

All of my girlfriends were happily married at this point, and I often felt like the odd woman out.

I went into hiding and unhappily began to plan my life as a single woman.

Then, three years later as I exited the subway station, I saw him standing there in front of his place of business. So cute and hot. For the first time in so long I was attracted to someone.

We looked at each other and I felt that the chemistry might be happening both ways.

Sure enough, he asked me to lunch, and we began dating. It was an unlikely long-term relationship. In no way did he fit my picture-image, but I felt excited about the possibility of a summer fling.

We have now been married for thirty-nine years. I learned that it's way better to wait long than to marry wrong.

My best advice is to focus on and develop yourself. Find things that bring you personal joy. Be open to new people and experiences. Never, ever stop believing that he/she is out there. Let the universe bring you both together.

Long Island Railroad
Jodi & Todd

8

I WAS JUST ENDING A lengthy and brutal divorce. My inner thought was: Who would want me?

I have old baggage and wounds. I have two daughters ages two and four. I will never go through this again. I will remain single. I will never remarry.

I was, however, lonely, and I hurt the most on the nights my ex took our daughters out to dinner. I decided to go online and find a dinner companion for those nights.

Todd, a confirmed bachelor, and I exchanged online emails, but we never met. He was frightened off by my having children since he was never getting married and certainly not to a woman with children!

Many months later, I was on the Long Island Railroad on my way home from work. Out of the blue I got a text from Todd. I replied that I couldn't talk since I was on the railroad. He said, "What car are you in?" What?

He was on the same train, two cars behind me.

He came to my car, and we got acquainted. Not only was that meeting serendipitous but on top of that we found out that we shared the very same birthday a few years apart.

We dated for a year. I told no one about him since it wasn't going to be anything permanent.

I liked everything about him.

He is the best man I know but I had to end it. I told him he had been a fantastic distraction but now I was ready to love again.

We parted. He was still not getting married.

A month later he called. He confessed to being in love and met my kids and family, and I met his.

Six months later we were married. That was nine years ago. He is totally devoted to my children. They adore him. He is the best stepfather and role model that I could have hoped for.

One of the very best things that happened besides the obvious of finding our love partners, was his mother saying to me that she waited for fifty years to bring a woman into our family and now we have three!

My best advice is to be true to yourself. Keep growing, loving yourself, and keep open to possibilities. My love came out of the blue and so can yours!

BATHROOM TO BOYFRIEND
Melody & Justin

I BEGRUDGINGLY AGREED TO GO with a friend on a trip to London to recover from a three-month broken heart.

I felt like I would never smile again. I was finished. No more dating for this girl. Too many disappointments and too many bad experiences. My heart hurt. I was going to focus solely on my career with a huge promotion in sight.

I had a wonderful time being a tourist in London without any interest in the men, even if they flirted.

Along with exploring this wonderful city, we went to the theater, had spa treatments, massages, and manicures. It was a true self-care indulgent long weekend. I loved and needed the pampering.

I was having a wonderful time despite feeling down and out over the breakup. It was also a relief. I needed that break from reality.

I was on a slow-moving line to the bathroom on the plane going home.

A handsome gentleman was sitting on an aisle seat reading a book that I had just finished. I told him that I read the book and loved it.

We had a little banter back and forth: What part are you up to? Are you enjoying it?... But it was cut short because darn, it was my turn to go to the bathroom.

I remember giggling to myself that shockingly, I was starting to find men attractive again. At least that one.

Little did I know that I'd just met the person I was supposed to be with for the rest of my life!

On my way back to my seat, Mr. Book Man tapped on my sleeve and said, "I'd love to continue our discussion. Here's my card and if you are comfortable, I'd love yours too."

We have been discussing books for fourteen years now and even read on our honeymoon.

Women, never throw in the towel. Men are everywhere, even on those days when we can't seem to see them.

" The beauty of love is that you can fall into it with the most unexpected person at the most unexpected time. "

~Ritu Ghatourey

Want to Hear a Joke?

Claire & Michael

AT FIFTY-FOUR AND SINGLE for thirteen very long years, I was so ready to meet that special someone whom I could spend the next passage of my life with.

I was out of fresh ideas on how to meet after seemingly exhausting all the men still breathing in the personals.

At that same time, I was a member of a women's group. They knew me very well and of my longing and readiness to meet him.

At one of our monthly meetings, they suggested, very strongly, that I get down on my knees and seriously ask for what I wanted. I literally got down on all fours and screamed to the universe, "I'm really, really, ready—please help me."

One of our members was the editor of the magazine where the most popular personal ads were placed (before the internet). She decided to create a lavish event. A dance to honor all the singles who used the magazine. The first one ever.

She asked us to do her a huge favor and help fill it up. Five of us went to support her.

Did I want to go? Absolutely not. But to support my friend, I went. I was feeling a little awkward and a bit shy, so I decided that instead of waiting for men to approach me, I would turn the tables and devise a plan to approach them.

I did a little man joke research and equipped myself with

three terrific jokes that were a little silly and a little risqué.

My master plan was working. I approached any man who looked somewhat interesting and said, "Would you like to hear a joke?" It was foolproof. They all said yes. I was batting 1.000 and received four phone calls the very next day.

And then, as I was walking up the staircase...he was walking down. The disco light was flashing on him, and I felt a shock throughout my body.

I stopped and said, "Would you like to hear a joke?" Michael laughed at all three and then said that he was so glad that I'd stopped him as he was a little shy and uncomfortable at large events.

We never stopped dancing and never stopped dating. Yes, we married and had a beautiful twelve-year marriage until, sadly, he passed away, seventeen years after the night of the jokes.

My advice is to take risks, get out of your comfort zone, don't be controlled by your negative inner voice telling you it's not going to happen for you.

THREE YEARS LATER
Nancy & Mike

11

AFTER A DISAPPOINTING LONG-TERM relationship went sour, I was extremely discouraged.

I wanted to go to the next step and get engaged, but sadly he didn't.

He wasn't ready so I had to come to terms with that fact. I ended the relationship.

There was absolutely no one else of interest. Hopeless, I accepted a blind date with a guy named Mike, with a girlfriend and her husband. We had a nice time, but he never called again.

And then, yes, I did. I went back with the former unavailable-for-marriage boyfriend. After a year I came to my senses and finally realized that it was over...for good.

Sad and depressed, I began to do what singles do. I went online (unsuccessfully), danced my tush off at singles dances, and had many fix-ups.

I was frustrated. I hadn't met anyone of substance, so I decided to just enjoy my life. I went out with friends, traveled, boosted my own self-esteem, and enjoyed my life without the added pressure of finding my soul mate.

Three years later, guess who asked my friend if I was single? Mike, the blind date who never called again.

We began to go out on dates once a week. I had been so

hurt in the past that I kept him at a distance.

I just wanted to have a good time. After celebrating our first anniversary, I realized that I was caring more than I thought I should and maybe it was time to end it.

My clock was now ticking, and I wanted a husband and family.

He was totally shocked and didn't want our relationship to end. So, he stepped up to the plate. Soon after, he told me that he loved me, proposed, and we never looked back.

We were married in 2000 and have a seventeen-year-old daughter.

Stop putting pressure on yourself. Enjoy your life. Be patient. Fulfill yourself with friends and interests.

Make it a great life with or without a man and trust that love will happen when it's supposed to.

12

Meeting the One to Father My Child
Donna & John

I met John in the middle of a very personal dark night of my soul. I was at my wit's end regarding my search for love.

I had dated to exhaustion, read every dating book, attended an entire series of classes on *Understanding Men*, and even went on the VH1 dating reality show *Tough Love* to find out what was wrong with me.

I was labeled "Ticking Clock" because I was forty, single, and had a deep calling to be a mother. It was a silly name, but accurate.

I felt my body ticking, and it flavored my entire dating experience. I needed some intensive repair, so I started a yoga challenge that brought me to a weekend workshop.

It was at this workshop that I first met John, the man who would be my husband and the father of my greatest miracle love, my daughter, Paloma June.

Within the first five minutes of meeting, John and I felt strangely connected, already bonding on the most random things.

He felt like home, like someone I already knew but had to learn everything about. He wasn't like anyone I'd ever met before.

That first night after the session had finished, he invited me to dinner. In a cozy booth, he boldly declared two things:

"I don't understand this, but I feel love for you," and simply, "I have this feeling I am going to know you for a really long time."

The second day of the workshop, we met early for coffee and brought our yoga mats. Just like me, John had a daily yoga practice, so while the other attendees went to lunch, we decided to hang back to do a short yoga sequence.

There he was doing his beautiful moves, and as he took his shirt off to do handstand pushups, I think I felt my entire body sigh. Where had he been all my life? I had just turned forty-one the week before, and he was forty-six.

I felt all my fears dissipate and knew that he was going to be my life partner. He is.

My advice is to keep your heart open on every level. Expand your dating pool, work on your inner core, tell your truth. And remember that it only takes one guy.

13

The Elevator
Susan & Marty

I HAD RECENTLY MOVED INTO the city motivated by the thought that at sixty-nine and divorced for eleven years there would be more opportunities to meet men and begin dating again.

I registered with an online dating site, and after a while I was very discouraged and disappointed with the men I was meeting. I was also weary and leery of the dating game and running low on trust.

I decided no more dating sites for me. I felt relieved and empowered and thought I would ask my friends to help me in my search for love.

Well, that did not work out so well. I threw up my hands and said that's it for me and the dating scene.

Serendipitous love did not ring my doorbell. It was waiting for me in the elevator. It was the night of my daughter's wedding rehearsal dinner. And, I have to say, I was looking very good, dressed in a fabulous jumpsuit and ready to dance and laugh the night away.

Love was in the air. I pressed the elevator button, not knowing this button would change my life. The doors parted and standing there was a nice-looking man I had not seen in the building before.

He looked at me and said, "Wow, you look beautiful."

We chatted for eight floors. When the doors opened in

the lobby, he said, "After you."

I replied, "No, after you."

"I am a gentleman, so it is definitely, after you." He then motioned for me to enter the lobby.

My hesitation to proceed him was all because on my own, I was not able to fully zip my jumpsuit and I knew it was noticeable.

As I turned to exit, he said, "Woah...I think you need some assistance with that zipper." Up the zipper went—along with my heartbeat.

I like this guy, I thought. Even though he was not my type, his personality was infectious, and he had delighted me for eight floors!

We parted ways that evening but became good friends. I began to realize I could trust him and what I was feeling was more than just friends.

We fell deeply in love. He was loving, caring, and an all-around great guy. And he made me laugh.

Sadly, we had less than a year together before he died. It was a year of wonderful vacations, sharing friends and family, and many romantic evenings, just the two of us.

My advice to women who want love in their lives is to always stay open and give the man you thought was not your type a chance. At the end of the day, all you need is love!

Rock Bottom to Romance
Danna & Michael

I GOT MARRIED AT A very young age, a month from nineteen, an unheard-of age to get married in the '80s.

We tried to defy the odds of a teenage marriage. Sadly, after twenty years it ended turbulently. When the marriage was finally over, I thought I would never be able to find someone ever again.

I was thrown into the single life, having very little experience. I was so naïve at almost forty.

Months later, I decided to start a serious relationship with someone I knew from the hospital where we worked together when I was a staff nurse and he was an attending physician. We had so much in common, both being in healthcare.

I thought maybe this would be someone I could live the rest of my life with. But we had different goals and different visions of our future together. After four and half years, I wanted a commitment, and he was not able to give me one.

My self-esteem was at rock bottom. I needed to take inventory on my actions, how my life was going, and where I wanted to be.

I needed to find my voice. We were at the point of no return and the relationship was pretty much over. I was just hanging on for no reason.

I avoided his calls. I avoided saying out loud that we were over.

I hated that I had another failed relationship. I was devastated.

One night I was on Facebook and came across a post from a friend and former co-worker from the hospital. I saw her brother had commented on her post.

Her brother was someone I had first met many years ago when I was still married. He was a really nice guy. I would set him up with my single nurse friends and we would all go out together socially.

When I was married, I would always think that if I met him when I was single, I would have loved to date him. I thought, What do I have to lose? I decided to friend him.

He never responded to the request. I decided to message his sister and ask what the problem was. Later I was told she called him and asked him, "What are you thinking?!" Because she knew he had always liked me.

He privately messaged me and stated he did not recognize my name. I had changed it back to my maiden name and he only knew me by my married name. He also didn't recognize my profile picture because I used one from high school. I responded. No sooner had I hit send, my phone rang.

We talked for hours. It was as if time stood still. We went to dinner the following week. We enjoyed each other's company, just like we did many years ago. I thought we were going to remain as friends, way back when.

Currently we have been dating for ten-plus years. He asked me to marry him a few months after we started dating. Even though I will not get married again, I will remain engaged. It's a wonderful place to be. I'm so very happy.

Looking back, I thought my relationships with men would never transpire into a long-term commitment because of my failed marriage and then my failed long-term relationship.

Obviously, I was wrong.

Never throw in the towel. Anything is possible, especially when you least expect it!

" The best relationships are the
ones you never saw coming. "

~ *Unknown*

BRAIN TUMOR

Sophia & Cyrus

I'VE ALWAYS HAD MEN IN my life. Even when we ended relationships, we remained good friends. I was very happy about that.

I was having vision problems and as a TV producer, my job was affected. When I went to an ophthalmologist, he was concerned that I had a brain tumor that was pressing on my optic nerve, creating vision problems.

He suggested that I contact a neuro-ophthalmologist. Although I lived in a big city, there were very few high-level surgeons who specialized in these areas.

The first two doctors that I was referred to didn't take my insurance, so I kept looking. How lucky was I that they didn't?

The third came highly recommended, and that's when my life changed. Brain tumor aside, I was about to meet the love of my life at forty-five.

I went to the appointment with a boyfriend who I was ready to break up with but kept him in the friend zone.

I immediately thought Dr. C was fantastic, intelligent, kind, attentive. And oh how cute he was!

When my friends called from Italy and asked about my tumor, all I could talk about was how handsome and caring my doctor was.

There for me the day of the surgery were my ex-husband, my current boyfriend, my daughter, and other friends.

Doc C later told me that he was so impressed by the amount of people who showed up for my surgery. He said it showed how loved and cared about I was and that is one of the things that he fell in love with about me.

The surgery was a huge success. He had me come back to his office for a follow-up checkup the next week.

I was all dressed up for a previous business appointment that morning, and I was wearing a beautiful dress with high heels. He was wowed. Most people dress down to go to doctors' visits. I was all dolled up. He asked me to have a celebratory drink.

After the doctor/patient relationship ended, we began to date. We are so very compatible, we have many similar interests and really like, as well as love, one another.

It's almost ten years now. My vision is still corrected so I now can see my honey with new and improved eyes. He gets more handsome and loving each year.

You never know. It happens everywhere when you least expect it, like me, going to check out my brain tumor and unexpectedly finding love. It can show up in the most serendipitous ways!

16

Small Town
Anna Lee & Van

Living in a small town, the pickings are slim as far as dating is concerned. Everyone knows everyone, or so I thought. Our paths had never crossed—until they did.

Divorced for five years with two small children, I was actually enjoying my freedom. It was a little shocking to me that I was so okay with being alone with the children. I was having a good time dating but I knew that I did want to meet someone special...eventually, but not at that time. No rush.

Little did I know how it would occur.

I had a friend who was also a friend to both Van and his then wife. I was out to dinner with her when she spotted them in a restaurant, and she went over to say hello. I didn't go over, so we never formerly met.

Months later, Van was divorced, and I was on a double date with our mutual friend and her date. Introductions were made all around.

Van asked my friend for my number. I was definitely interested but he didn't call.

My friend ran into him again and asked if he had called, even though she knew he didn't.

He replied, "I lost her number." A likely story. I still don't really know to this day, forty years later.

She gave it to him again. Surprisingly, he called. We had a

lovely lunch, which led to a wonderful deep connection.

What I was attracted to besides his good looks was how comfortable he was to speak with, how interesting he was, that he was a great listener, and that he had the patience of a saint.

We never looked back and have been married for forty years. And it works. We both are committed to making one another happy.

My advice is to let life take its course, be happy right where you are, and remain open to serendipitous meetings!

17

IDENTICAL TWIN
Desiree & Matthew

I WAS DIVORCED, A SINGLE mom to a young daughter and a businesswoman. I was fulfilled.

I loved being a mom, successful and happy with my career choice.

I chose to devote myself to this life and not date until my daughter was in an out-of-town college, and yet I was certain that I wanted romantic love in my life.

Off she went. Look out world, here I come, ready and willing to meet my love partner.

I was on hold all those years yet still feeling attractive and youthful.

Nothing was going to stop me until I found him. Oh, and I was in my very late fifties.

Shortly after, I met a divorced man whom I was attracted to who was an identical twin (important part of my story).

Mel and I both had good heads for business and so we decided to partner in a side business. We were creating events for singles.

Joyfully, it was starting to take off. The future was looking good.

A bunch of friends decided to rent a summer place and we both took shares.

Here comes the sad part. On Memorial Day weekend (the

first weekend of our season) he broke it off.

He said that he couldn't combine business and plea-sure.... I said, "Forget the business," and he said no.

Oh how unhappy I was at the time and oh how happy I am now that it didn't work out.

·Meet Matthew, his identical twin brother who came to one of our events.

As soon as we met, I could tell the difference between the brothers. I really liked this brother. We had a great very long conversation but no date.

Months later, the same thing happened and again we talked into the night. Again, no date!

Finally, he texted me and said that he was recently sepa-rated and not ready for anything serious.

I was on a fast track to get serious with someone and he was not. I was the hare and he was the tortoise. Another disappointment.

We became very good friends without benefits.

And then by sheer accident I literally fell in the street and broke my pelvis. Guess who stayed in a chair next to my bed for two nights in the hospital and brought me chicken soup?

Yes. Matthew! That's where the amazing shift happened. He was so very attentive, loving, and caring and I was falling deeply in love. And...so was he.

It was worth waiting for and we confessed our love. He moved in shortly after that. It only took three years, LOL!

We have been together for eleven years. The right twin serendipitously came into my life.

Never ever give up. Keep the faith. Fill your head with positive thoughts. Just because there's no love interest when you wake up tomorrow doesn't mean there won't be an unex-pected meeting by the evening.

18

THE RESUME
Cheryl & Howard

I PULLED INTO MY PARENTS' driveway, turned off the motor, and stared at the house I grew up in. The house was empty. Like me, I thought.

I was in my head the whole five-hour drive. The recurring thought was: *Why am I still with this man who does not want anything serious, including children, which I do want?*

There has to be a new relationship out there for me and a new job.

I'm smart, funny, and ambitious and I want a man I can share that with. And I want to make enough money in a new job to support my dreams, whether in or out of a relationship.

I had, just that week, heard about an IT job that seemed interesting. I was indecisive about whether I should send in my resume because the location was well over an hour drive, and in Los Angeles commuting time, it was really a two-hour drive. *No, I cannot spend four hours a day on the freeway.*

But the job kept nagging at me, so I addressed and stamped an envelope with my resume and left it on the hall table, on the other side of the table from the stack of stamped bills to mail.

Therein lies the serendipitous moment that would change my life.

Darn, I forgot to mail my bills. I called and asked my

roommate to mail the bills for me ASAP.

Well, she scooped up all the envelopes, including the re-sume, and off it went to a job I wasn't totally convinced that I wanted.

They called and I went for an interview. I went knowing I really did not want this job. The drive was unforgiving. But the interview was going well. When asked about salary, I boldly asked for an unrealistic amount, knowing that was my out.

Two months passed and one day, unexpectedly, they called and offered me the job and they met my financial request.

One week later I began the job. Little did I know that that one decision would completely alter my life—for the rest of my life.

On my second day, I was introduced to Howard. Smart, tall, handsome (loved how he dressed), and kind. He would be training me over the next couple of weeks.

The alarm and the happy bells all went off at the same time. He was flirting with me, and I could not resist a flirt back. He asked me out. *Better not go* was my first thought. Office romance has consequences. Howard quickly dispelled that thought and proceeded in his pursuit—of me.

Howard continued to dispel my fears of an office ro-mance, and he also restored my faith and trust in a relation-ship and in love.

I am so happy that he persisted, and so are our three amazing children. They are all smart, tall, and beautiful, just like their dad.

I say, keep your mind and heart open to all possibilities, whether or not they fit the photos in your head. Having a checklist keeps you lonely.

Is This Seat Taken?
Gloria & Jon

I COMMUTED INTO GRAND CENTRAL out of the Riverdale train station daily, after dropping my son off at nursery school.

When you take the same train every morning you befriend commuters and chitchat on the way in. I met a woman, Louise, and we would talk about our husbands and how unhappy we both were in our marriages.

There was a very handsome commuter who sat with us too, but we didn't talk to him. She and I were sharing too many tales like two little girls chatting away.

Saying I was unhappy led me to many excursions that I am not proud to even remember—but the bottom line was I was feeling unloved and looking for love in all the wrong places.

On Administrative Professionals Day (formerly referred to as National Secretaries Day), I placed the beautiful flowers my boss had given me on the vacant seat next to me.

On this particular and life-changing day, I was commuting home from my office, when the handsome commuter from the morning commute stopped and asked me, "Is this seat taken?"

I practically threw the flowers on the floor to make room for him.

We both told each other we were happily married. After

following weeks of talking and lying to each other, he finally shared that he was unhappily married and I boasted with joy, "So am I."

I fell deeply in love with that handsome commuter, who today is my husband of thirty-seven years.

They said it would never last because of our circumstances. The odds were against us. But I decided to give love a second chance. Why?

Through a lot of self-discovery, self-care, and accepting my self-worth, I realized that I deserved it.

To make this relationship successful, we both had a great deal of soul searching to do. Through self-reflections and wonderful outside help, I worked very hard on myself.

I first had to find that love in me—before I could accept that someone else could love me.

From "Is this seat taken?" to a strong, committed, long-lasting love affair has been one of life's greatest gifts!

"You're my serendipity. I wasn't looking for you, I wasn't expecting you, but I'm very lucky I met you."

~Unknown

THE RIGHT NUMBER
Sandra & Cosmos

M<small>Y MARRIAGE OF FOURTEEN YEARS</small> fell apart. No reason why it should have. We had all the ingredients for the perfect formula. We graduated college together, were of the same religion, and we shared a deep friendship in addition to love.

His job took us overseas to live in Hong Kong for four years, and we immersed ourselves in the experience. After returning home the rug was pulled out from under me. My best description is that I felt like I was walking around on one leg. Part of me was missing; my whole being was off-balance.

After a long while, I knew I didn't want to marry again, but meeting, relating, and sharing was still very important to my wholeness. With my wings spread, this time the ingredients didn't have to be perfect, and in several cases, they were anything but perfect.

However, each of those relationships exposed me to different horizons and I don't regret any one of them. The best thing to come out of that period was that I was ready to commit, on my terms.

One November Thursday morning, twenty-three years ago, at 6:30 a.m., I entered my chiropractor's office for my bimonthly maintenance adjustment.

I went at that time because I was able to be adjusted, come home, and ditch the sweats for work clothes and still catch a train to New York City.

Upon entering my chiropractor's office that particular morning, I came face to face with a very tall, broad man, reminiscent of one who played football twenty years prior. He unashamedly stared at me until I was called into the room for my treatment.

Later that day I received a call from the chiropractor who told me the gentleman bombarded him with questions. "What's her name, Doc? What can you tell me about her, Doc?"

Of course, the doctor replied that he could share no information other than I came to his office every other Thursday at the same time.

And there he was, two weeks later when I arrived for my appointment, filling up the office space. We talked, he asked for my number, and I gave it.

That evening my phone rang. When I answered, the first thing he said was, "It's really you. I had myself prepared for you giving me an incorrect number."

As we shared our stories, he told me he was working in the area on a transfer from Chicago and was a divorced father of three daughters. I also came to learn that this giant of a man was not afraid to shed tears when he talked about them.

We started a two-year relationship until he was transferred back home.

We are now in a committed relationship, albeit long distance. We can tell you the pluses and minuses of every airline between Newark and O'Hare.

We miss each other when we're apart, and love and laugh ferociously when we reunite. On the occasions when we do discuss cohabitating in one city or the other, we both come to the same conclusion—what we have is so special we wouldn't want to tarnish it by taking it for granted or having it become mundane. Obviously, this situation is not for everyone, but for us it's a precious gift.

After experiencing the emotional trauma of a fractured love affair, you will most probably want to cocoon and protect yourself from any more hurt. While that is necessary for personal healing, it is most important to remain positive about yourself.

My Teenage Crush
Paige & Ethan

I WAS PINCHING MYSELF FOR days over landing an amazing job on Fire Island. I was to spend the summer as a mother's helper to adorable eight-year-old twin girls.

At fourteen, I felt incredibly lucky to spend the summer on a gorgeous island and play on the beach with easygoing and fun-loving girls. A big bonus was being welcomed by a warm and loving family.

After a few days, magic happened! Ethan, their nineteen-year-old brother, came home from a college in Boston.

I could feel the immediate flush on my face when we were introduced. Did they all see it too? He was not only easy on the eyes but wore a huge grin and had a wonderful sense of humor. My kind of guy.

I was not at all cool at that age. I wore my heart on my sleeve. To him, I was just a cute kid.

He was only going to be on the island for a few days since he had a summer job as a counselor at a camp in Maine. He made quite the lasting impression on me in those few days. I made it very clear that I wanted him to be my guy when we got older.

The whole family teased me in a loving way. Ethan never made me feel uncomfortable, although there was no way he could avoid my adoring gaze.

The following summer I saw him for a short visit before he left for camp. More than ever, I was absolutely sure I was going to marry him.

I flirted like crazy but now he was a man of twenty, and I was still that kid to him at fifteen. No progress was made.

In my senior year of college, I met the man who would become my husband and I forgot about my massive crush on Ethan. I heard that he was married as well, although the family and I had lost touch.

My marriage was challenging right from the start. We were not a good match. Our listening skills needed work. We were oil and water. We married too young.

After nine years we decided that we grew too far apart and divorced. It was painful. I was down and out.

I learned a great deal about myself, and I was smart enough to know not to jump back into a new relationship.

I was not ready to date. The thought of kissing someone right then was not in the cards, but I didn't want to wait too long since I was in my thirties and wanted to be a mom. It was a dilemma.

The best thing I did for myself was to see a therapist and took a pause as far as dating was concerned.

After a year of self-reflection and personal growth, I knew I was ready to venture out into the dating pool again.

But how could I ever meet someone? I was opposed to online dating and didn't go to bars. Was I too old?

I signed up for an adult education psychology course, and when the professor came in, I almost fell off my chair! It was my Ethan!

At thirty-two, I felt the same feelings come over me as they did at fifteen.

Would he recognize me? It was seventeen years later. He wouldn't remember me. Or would he?

Ethan did a roll call. When he came to my name (I went back to using my maiden name), he looked quizzical, looked up, caught my eye, and broke out into a huge smile.

We met after class and had coffee that lasted three hours.

The planets were in alignment. The feelings and sparks were flying. This time they were reciprocated.

Everything was right. He too was divorced and living not too far from me in Connecticut.

This story has a very happy ending. It was totally unexpected and worth waiting for.

My crush, my first love, is now my husband and it's so right. I can't wait until our two girls are old enough to hear the story of how we met—again!

We think we can control our future, but we can't. The best we can do is enjoy the moments that we are given. Make the very best of them.

Don't get too discouraged because life has its ways of surprising us. Remember, patience is a virtue.

22

DATING DURING COVID
Sharna & Gary

AFTER A THIRTY-THREE-YEAR marriage to a guy seven years younger than me, I came to the painful conclusion that it was time to move on.

At sixty-five-years-old, that was a terrifying thought!

I had retired, we moved to Panama, and a year later he returned to the US. Here I was, a single and older woman in Panama.

Not likely that I would meet someone that was compatible. After all, don't all the guys my age prefer someone younger? Arm candy?

And I was not looking for someone who would slow me down. I am blessed with good health, physical fitness, and joie de vivre.

My technical career background includes sales and marketing, and I knew how to sell a product!

So, I got busy, my age be damned. I could make something happen.

In early November of 2018, I decided I didn't want to spend New Year's Eve alone. A little voice (my Jewish mother's maybe?) told me to call my cousin and book a Jewish singles cruise with her company.

I had traveled with her before when she launched her business twenty years ago and allowed my then husband and me to travel with her singles group to help get things going.

Now that I was single again, I could travel with her tour company legitimately.

I booked a two-week cruise from Buenos Aires, around the horn and ending in Santiago, Chile. I was not thinking about meeting anyone but at least I would be with family to ring in 2019.

And, of course, there I met Gary, a retired veterinarian with a career in research and the intent to live this next chapter of life to the fullest.

He came to visit me in Panama shortly after the cruise ended. We had a very nice three weeks getting to know one another and he departed for home to assist his brother with tax season.

His plan was to return in eight weeks for a longer stay. Then COVID hit and Panama's borders were sealed.

Although I didn't see Gary for almost nine months, we spoke every evening for three or four hours.

He finally returned to Panama mid-October of last year. Now a year has gone by, and both of our lives have changed dramatically.

We bought a farm and expanded our family adding another dog to my two, two cats, and another horse.

Our wedding will be this coming February.

Gary has never been married and was determined to enjoy a Jewish married life for the duration. So, now he will have that. And I will too.

Final act? We don't see it that way. Just another chapter for two adventurers aged sixty-nine (me) and seventy-one (Gary).

23

UN-RUSTY
Ann & Bill

ALL BUSINESS, BILL HAD WALKED into my empty new apartment and surveyed the scene. "Hi, I am Bill from The Container Store, and I am here to measure your closets."

Tall, slender, silver-haired, goateed, wearing a white button-down and khakis, Bill was easily the most distinguished tradesman I had ever seen.

Without any logical explanation for why my brain processed the feeling, I was instantly attracted and needed to know more about this man.

Maybe it was that I was newly arrived in New York from decades in Texas, and that my old life had just ended.

"I have closets in three rooms that need measuring. How long will that take you?" (I had a date!)

Once he surveyed the scope of work, I quickly got the answer. He couldn't possibly complete the measures in time for me to cross town to meet my dinner date.

"Would you compromise and stay to finish after I leave?"

What happened next would have in most circumstances signaled the end of our encounter. I gave my thanks, announced I must go, and offered to leave the air conditioning on. I asked Bill to text me images of the remaining closets when he finished.

Several hours later, an unknown cell number and message

appeared on my phone.

"Thank you for the air conditioning. I turned it off and locked the door. Enjoy your new life in Manhattan. Here are your drawings."

"Thank you so much," I answered, "and for the good wishes on my new life. It's either going to be daunting or fun to be single in Manhattan."

Within minutes came back his answer. "It's going to be FUN!!!" What?? He used all caps and three exclamation points. Could this be the same taciturn man I had just met?

I responded: "How do you know it will be fun? Are you single? Do you live in the City?"

His reply thrilled me: "Yes, I am single. I used to live in the City. And it was fun!!"

Two weeks and two days later we met. With a last-minute cancellation, Bill was free for lunch and the rest of the afternoon.

We said hello. And I felt it again—that unnamed chemistry. I thought I saw intrigue in his eyes when he looked back at me.

I learned later that he had debated with himself whether he should meet me at all. He had seriously thought about telling me he had a girlfriend. Why? Because he hadn't had a date in five years. Working six days a week, on a very tight budget, and after a failed relationship, he was almost convinced that meeting women wasn't worth the effort ever again.

The next five and a half hours flew by. After the date, Bill shouldered his backpack. "Not so fast," I said. "I don't know if I'll ever see you again. So, I am going to kiss you."

Bill's face blanched white as I leaned up to press my lips on his. He barely kissed back. "I apologize," he said. "I am afraid I am very rusty."

"Well, then, we are going to try that one more time," I countered. I leaned in and kissed him again, a little longer.

That move to kiss Bill was a year ago, an anniversary that coincides with my move to Manhattan. In both of those decisions, I have found grace, untold surprises, and a new life.

And I've learned how to make a skeptical man un-rusty, and that downsizing your material possessions can mean up-sizing your life.

24

THE PROPHECY
Mark & Debbie

"MARK, YOU ARE GOING TO meet and marry a woman who works in a hospital!"

Rita, a wonderful tea leaf reader and renowned psychic, came into my life through a recommendation by a coworker, whom I highly respected.

I had never done anything like this before.

I kept myself open to trying all new things because I was so ready to meet a special woman. I had been divorced for three years and I absolutely knew that I wanted to remarry and have children.

Rita was smart and centered—not "woo-woo" at all. I was pleasantly surprised and felt comfortable at once.

Mark, she said, "You are going to meet the woman you are going to marry, a woman who works in a hospital, by January of 1988." It was now 1987.

I took her words very seriously. I had a year to find my forever love.

After this reading, Rita and I stayed in touch, and she fixed me up a few times.

Although nice, they weren't the one, and none of them worked in a hospital.

The next time I heard from Rita, she excitedly told me that she gave my number to a fantastic woman named Debbie and to expect a phone call. And yes, she worked in a hospital as a social worker!

As fate would have it, I never knew that she called. Back in the day, we didn't have cell phones and I was having trouble with my answering machine.

I never received her message. Rita was clear that this was a meeting that had to happen. She suggested that I call her—ASAP!

At the same time, my mother, who was a French teacher, would often talk about her favorite student Paul, a great guy whom I met a few times because my mom kept in contact with him.

Mom, knowing the psychic's prediction and wanting her son to be happy, suggested that I meet Paul's sister, whom she had met and thought was fantastic.

"No, Mom."

"But she works in a hospital," she said.

"No, Mom, I'm not interested."

I most definitely did not want my mother finding me a wife.

We didn't know it at the time, but it was the very same Debbie, the social worker.

What are the chances? A little luck, a little pinch of coincidence, mixed with a cup of serendipity brought us together.

We had our first lunch right before our time ran out. It was in December of 1987, one month before Rita's cutoff date!

I knew within the first ten minutes that we were going to get married. She was everything I was looking for. Bright and beautiful, interesting, and interested.

We married nine months later and have been a happy couple with two children for thirty-five years.

Be open to anything that may be out of your comfort zone. I did and it was the best thing that ever happened to me.

66 Sweet Serendipity, that
unexpected meeting that
changes your life. 99

~Alexa

Photos
of
Couples

2 ~ Kate & Arthur

3 ~ Pamela & Neil

4 ~ Jill & Dennis

5 ~ Laura & Miguel

6 ~ *Barbara & Steve*

7 ~ *Ellie & Gary*

8 ~ Jodi & Todd

10 ~ Claire & Michael

11 ~ Nancy & Mike

12 ~ Donna & John

14 ~ Danna & Michael

19 ~ Gloria & Jon

23 ~ Ann & Bill

28 ~ Judy & Jerome

31 ~ Debra & Jack

32 ~ Sheila & Al

33 ~ Randee & Alan

35 ~ Nikki & Leonard

36 ~ Susan & Bruce

37 ~ Bev & Jeff

38 ~ Liz & Daryl

40 ~ Zöe & Wil

43 ~ Jill & Don

44 ~ Connie & Jim

47 ~ Ana & Michael

48~ Nora & Tom

25

ALWAYS A BRIDESMAID
Samantha & Paul

YES, I WAS THE STEREOTYPICAL "always a bridesmaid...never a bride" kinda girl.

Yes, I had a closet full of awful-looking dresses that I'd never wear again.

Yes, I was happy for my friends.

Yes, I too wanted to be a bride.

And yes, I took myself on a honeymoon.

I had recently seen a movie where the main character was fed up with always buying gifts for friends' showers, engagements, and weddings.

She decided to give herself a lavish gift and take herself on a vacation with a brand-new attitude, and most important, to celebrate herself.

What led to my having a brand-new attitude was that I'd recently attended a workshop with a very impressive relationship therapist, whom after two hours of inspiring over one hundred single women said. "Raise your hand if you would like to be in a love relationship and you're not."

We all raised our hands.

"Maybe, just maybe, the type you think is your type is not your type," she said.

And then she surprised us by saying, "I'd like to introduce you to my husband."

Out came a man who was at least a head shorter than her.

She then said, "As you can see, I'm not his type and he's not my type, on paper that is. What I'm here to tell you is that ours is the best relationship we know. We want to understand one another, we appreciate one another, we are always in gratitude for one another."

Hmmm...time to ditch the checklist that obviously wasn't working for me.

When I met Paul, my heart opened. I felt safe and known and he did too.

So off I went on my trip, this time without my list. No, I didn't meet anyone special, but I did have a great time. I came home refreshed and ready to meet new men.

Part of my new attitude was to tell *everyone* I knew that I was ready for love. *Everyone*, even the twenty-two-year-old receptionist at the dental office.

I never would have done that before. I took a stand for myself and was being proactive. I gave her my card and planted the message in her head.

Shortly after that interchange, she went to a family wedding and re-connected with her awesome uncle whom she hadn't seen in many years, since they lived in different states

He was a widower who had just moved back to my city, Chicago.

Then came the magical words from her uncle Paul. "I'm ready to meet someone special. Do you know anyone?" Bingo.

She later told me that she had no idea that I was single, and she never would have known to fix us up if I hadn't mentioned it.

The rest, as they say, is history. I am a bride, not a bridesmaid, and have been for the last seven years.

Of course, my advice is to tell everyone, even those who you would never think to tell, that you are ready to meet someone terrific, because *you* are!

26

TICK TOCK
Jennifer & David

I ALWAYS FELT EVERYONE AROUND could hear the ticking sound of my baby clock. It was so loud.

Ever since junior high school, I can remember thinking that all I wanted to do in life was to push a baby carriage.

That's one of the reasons I became a kindergarten teacher. Being around children and contributing to them was my higher purpose. I looked forward to seeing those beautiful little faces every day and couldn't wait to have my own.

At thirty-three, my heart was broken to smithereens...I heard the words that an engaged woman never wants to hear.

"After much soul searching, I decided that I don't think we should continue our relationship. I don't want children."

I was beyond crushed.

Four years of my life was wasted on someone who pretended to want what I wanted. He knew how important family was to me. We had spent endless hours discussing this.

It took me a long time to recover. First from the shock, then the disappointment. Then the fear engulfed me. *Would I ever have the partner and family I so craved?*

My dreams were shattered, and I had a clock to deal with.

After spending time hibernating and licking my wounds, I knew that what was most important was to find a true partner who wanted what I wanted, a family.

I did everything to meet men through the usual channels, but I wasn't having fun. It felt like work. I was scrutinizing every man to make sure that he was open to having children. In retrospect, that probably felt like a job interview to them, which was not good for romance.

It was meet the teacher day when a warm and friendly looking man named Dan came to see me.

His son Corey was in my kindergarten class. We had a lovely conversation about his son, and I found myself wondering, *Who is the lucky lady to be married to someone like him?*

He was just my type of guy. Perhaps he has a brother?

I found out later that he and his wife, Denise, were new to the neighborhood. His wife was in her ninth month of pregnancy, which is why we couldn't meet that day.

I finally met Denise, and we had a very special instant connection. They invited me to Corey's sixth birthday party.

My life changed that day the instant they introduced me to her brother, David.

Life has been wonderful ever since. The years of heartache were over. Our family values were an exact match. We have three children, the number we both wanted.

I went from the most hopeless, frightened, and discouraged person you could ever meet to someone whose dreams came true

That's my advice. Even in the bleakest moments, hold on tight to your dreams with hope and an open heart.

27
Don't Answer That Ad
Elizabeth & Ben

He did it again! He broke up with me for the second time.

We weren't married but we were talking about getting engaged.

He was the love of my life.

Was he frozen in fear? Cold feet? I was devastated. I could not go through this again.

After three months of a pure pity party, I came to my senses, and got myself to a good therapist.

After two months she told me that I didn't really need her. I was okay. But, she said, "Keep feeling your feelings. The grief process is tricky. It comes in waves when you least expect it."

What she suggested was that I get social again...not to rush into another relationship but just to get out of my head. I agreed. I had been a hermit for the last few months, which was not like me at all.

My plan was to put an ad in the personals (before we had online dating) in a popular magazine.

I also planned a trip to Club Med for a long Memorial Day weekend that was coming up.

At the time I was working for a magazine and knew many copywriters. I called my most talented and favorite to help me create my ad (he wrote it).

When I called to place it, the person on the other end of the phone was impressed. He said that I would do very well; it was so creative and different.

My ad began like this: *Forget every other woman on this page. I'm looking for what the scarecrow, the tin man, and the lion had.*

The day before my trip, the magazine came out. I began to scan the other ads (checking out my competition) when I saw a headline that stopped me in my tracks and gave me extra heartbeats.

The headline of the ad began with: *Are you woman enough?*

I knew it was his.

He spoke that way. The rest of the ad was even more of a giveaway.

His age, height, and weight were very specific. Mine was totally generic. My ad was not identifiable.

It was too unbelievable that both our ads were in the same issue, so I called the magazine. I spoke to the same person whom I had talked to the week before but because of confidentiality, he wasn't at liberty to tell me his name.

I then told him that I wanted to answer the ad but would be humiliated if it was his.

He said, "Just tell me his name and I'll tell you if you should answer his ad."

He got back on the phone and said, "All I can tell you is do not answer that ad."

It was rough. I fantasized about all the fabulous women he would be dating as I went off to Club Med with a very heavy heart.

I did have a good time socializing and knew at that point that I would be okay.

The phone rang early that next morning. It was Ben. We had not spoken in five months.

He claimed that he missed me and our fun and deep conversations.

After two hours he asked if we could continue these talks.

I said no, it would be way too painful.

Before we hung up, I said, "By the way, I saw your ad in *New York Magazine* and my ad is listed in the same issue. It was incredulous."

He then asked for my headline.

When we ended the call sadness engulfed me. I was still madly in love with this man. Why couldn't it have worked out?

Twenty minutes later, he called again.

This time he said, "Beth, it's bigger than both of us...we have to try again. I answered your ad!" Serendipity was operating at its finest.

In those days, the responses came in manilla envelopes ten days after the ads were placed, so we hadn't received ours until a few days later.

We were joyfully back together the next day. The responses arrived and we read them together. Holding hands, we deposited them in the trash.

Even on the bleakest of days, know that there is always hope...keep feeling your feelings and as a dear friend always says, *Relax and trust!*

28

Lessons and Love from a Ninety-Eight-Year-Old
Judy & Jerome

I THOUGHT THE RABBI WAS kidding. "You want to introduce me to a ninety-eight-year-old who wants to date?"

"No," he said, "I want to introduce you to a ninety-eight-year-old who would be open to getting remarried! His son came to ask me if I knew anyone exceptional."

At seventy-five, I was still youthful, cheerful, and happily engaged in running my business. However, I was at a point where online dating had led me to a string of men who continued to disappoint me.

I began to think maybe the sun had set on my romantic life. Then I met Jerome.

Before our first get-acquainted date, he had to cancel because he had a bad cold. "But," he said on my answering machine, "we will always have mañana."

And, for a time, it seemed as if we just might. His positive attitude, brilliance, wisdom, warmth, and charm captivated me completely.

He stood outside my building, the image of a perfect gentleman, when he came to pick me up for our first date—an evening on the town.

There he was, with a glow about him, so elegantly dressed, smiling, proudly relating that he had a great night planned for us.

Jerome did not look his age: he had a full head of hair, intense blue eyes, and the slim build of a former avid tennis player and golfer.

I would be lying if I said that I was not awed by the lifestyle he shared with me in our short four months together:

Our first date was magical, and he gave me a feather-light kiss good night. I treasured that kiss.

We had a complete connection and were able to take pleasure in each other in every way.

I was honored that he wanted to share so much of his life story with me. He talked almost nonstop: this titan of industry telling me how he built his business, describing all the events of his life, asking my opinion of things, and then really listening! He was a serious man, but he could also make me laugh.

Jerry asked me to move in with him—and I said yes, I would gladly do so when we got back after a blissful long weekend together.

We had so many exciting plans for the next few weeks and months.

The following day after he had asked me if we could live together, he was fatigued.

"I still feel like a teenage boy," he told me more than once. I believed him.

His ninety-ninth year was a few weeks away, with a big party planned. I felt sure he would make it to his centennial celebration.

The idea that he was soon to die never entered my mind. He had promised me mañana; in fact, many tomorrows. We had plans that stretched out for months, if not years.

No, this had to be a minor setback.

Sadly, he left this earth in a place he loved, never being an invalid, which he feared more than anything. He died fast, without pain, after a very long and wonderful life.

I was so privileged to have been with him even for a brief period and able to make him happy at the tag end of his charmed life.

I will never again feel his arms around me. I will miss

the way this brilliant man trusted me and confided in me. He made me feel worthy.

How do you move ahead from this kind of loss? Whether you have lost a lifelong spouse or another beloved family member or dear friend—or even someone who graced your life briefly but profoundly—death always wins.

I am not a woo-woo kind of person, but sometimes when the evidence is this clear you have to believe. The night after this remarkable man died, I lay on the bed in the room we had shared, eyes swollen shut from crying—and felt his hand in mine.

Having just lost this phenomenal man, I wonder if I can find another man to love.

Jerome had married the love of his life and spent forty-five beautiful years with her.

Four years after she died, we found each other. I asked him once if he thought we each have only one soul mate in a lifetime. He said no, that we could have more than one.

Then he added, "After my wife died—she as you know was a woman I adored beyond measure—I could have chosen to sit alone in a darkened room, pouring over photo albums.

"But why focus on what is lost when life is so precious?

"And," he smiled at me, "look what I found!"

So yes, I wish we could have borrowed even a bit more time. Nonetheless, I am grateful for what I received and what I was able to give him in those magical four months of our lives.

Love the life you live. Even if it's over when you turn one hundred, it will be over way too soon.

HAIRDRESSER SECRETS
29
Angela & Matt

ONE OF US SAID, "I don't know why we're still doing this," and the other replied, "I don't know either."

That was the week of my sixteenth wedding anniversary, and my husband (now ex) and I had an argument over a jar of salsa I had thrown away. That was the straw that broke the camel's back in our marriage.

We both knew that the time had come. It was inevitable and had been looming for a few years. Even so, we were both stunned.

It's very difficult to make the decision to walk away when nobody did anything wrong. There was nothing salacious. No cheating. No abuse of any kind. We had just become room-mates and neither of us wanted that for the rest of our lives.

Fast forward a few months. Our very amicable divorce was near the end point, and I was happily living alone in our home (with our son here half the time) and started dating.

I was ready and eager to move on and do things I really loved and had missed. Dating was fun! I embraced dating apps and met a few wonderful men. I dated each of them for about three months and, although I'm sure they have no idea, they all played a role in helping me heal.

I went into dating with the mindset that I was going to enjoy the men I dated for exactly who and what they were and not try to force it to be something it wasn't. It was a fabulous experience for me to date as a forty-eight-year-old successful professional who didn't want or need a free drink or free meal.

I also told myself after my divorce that, going forward, I would be unapologetically myself, even if that meant I was too much for some people.

Fast forward to July 2018. I had been divorced for nine months. My hairdresser had been with me through it all. She heard all the details of my life in the years leading up to my divorce and laughed with me as I regaled her with details of my dating life.

I was too much for my ex. When I started dating, I told every single man I met, I'm a lot. Looking back now I realize that it was a defense mechanism. I was giving them an out in the event that I was too much for them.

One day after my hairdresser came back to work after having her second baby, she was cutting my hair and we were chatting, as usual. She stopped what she was doing and looked at me in the mirror and said, "You know, Dr. R is divorced?"

I said that I didn't know that although I knew who he was because he had been my doctor a few years prior. And then she said six words that would change my life forever: "You guys would be amazing together."

Little did I know that Dr. R (Matt) had shared all the details of his divorce with my hairdresser. He had just delivered her baby four months prior, and she absolutely loved him.

And she was right. From the first date we realized that we are amazing together.

Matt and I got married on August 29, 2020, smack in the middle of COVID. Nothing was stopping us.

We are now six. He has three sons and my one, which makes for an interesting, fun, and loving blended family.

My thoughts: Don't try to turn every man you meet into marriage material because they're not. If you're open to it and don't put too much weight on it, dating experiences can be very light, fun, and healing.

Be willing to enjoy the relationships that come with dating for what they are and walk away when it no longer serves you. Be comfortable with who you are and embrace every bit of yourself.

“Love can be found in unexpected places. Sometimes we go out searching for what we think we want, and we end up with what we're supposed to have.”

~ *Kate McGahan*

30
LIFE IMITATING ART
Allison & David

I WAS AN ACTRESS, a young Jewish girl from Chicago, dating someone eighteen years older.

Someone who wasn't Jewish. Someone my parents didn't approve of on many levels. I loved him but I was unhappy that my parents and grandmother were so unhappy.

Coincidently, I was the lead actress in a play in Chicago that would soon be coming to Off Broadway in New York City. I was playing a Jewish schoolteacher from Chicago who was dating out of her faith—life imitating art at its finest.

In the play, to please her parents, she invents a boyfriend—a Jewish doctor. When the parents insist on meeting him, she hires an actor to play her pretend acceptable boyfriend. As the play unfolds, she falls in love with the hired actor.

Sophie, the actress playing my mother, also didn't like my boyfriend, whom she met on the set numerous times. He wasn't a bad guy, just too old for such a young girl, out of my faith, and we were in very different places in our lives.

Once Sophie found out that my mother felt the same way, she went into action.

She had her mind set on someone she thought was right for me.

It was her daughter-in-law's brother (yes, a Jewish

doctor) who had recently ended an engagement. She insisted that I just meet him once. I was a big NO!

Sophie paid no attention to my no and invited David to see the show. He came backstage and I was pleasantly surprised to meet a kind and quality man with beautiful, enchanting eyes.

A few days later, to be polite, I agreed to have a drink with him. He had a rose in hand and was quite charming—quite.

After the drink he called Sophie and proceeded to tell her that he was going to marry me!

I declined anything further because I still wanted to work on my existing relationship, but I was becoming more and more unhappy in it.

After time, I ended the relationship.

Sophie immediately let David know that I was available, but I wasn't ready to jump right into a new one.

Over the next few months, David began to woo me. He sent flowers, cards, and letters and continued to call.

I did feel a pull toward him, but I was feeling confused. This all seemed too easy.

I wanted to go slowly, which we did until David had an opportunity to go to London and Athens on a business trip. He wanted me to join him.

I was hesitant until my grandmother said, "You go on that trip," and she meant it.

I was still feeling uncomfortable on the trip, and the usually patient and kind David was now getting impatient.

He later told me that he was ready to give up pursuing me and made a plan. He was going to end this relationship, if I was still holding back, when we got home.

And then something shifted when I looked over and saw David sleeping on the plane. I felt a physical chill throughout my body.

I knew I couldn't let such a great man go.

I did not want to miss out on a future with this amazing man. When I finally surrendered, my fears dissipated, and I let myself show my love.

My gut instinct told me that I was going to marry this man!

And we did. It's been twenty-eight years. I still get butter-flies when I see him!

My advice is to allow yourself to let things happen, be open to all possibilities and to all signals, and let yourself receive.

31
PRIX FIXE DINNER
Debra & Jack

THE WEEKEND CONSISTED OF VISITING my parents, who live on Long Island, and doing loads of my laundry that wasn't so easy to do, since I lived in Manhattan.

It was a lovely winter weekend. I was on a serious hiatus from dating...at least until after the High Holidays in September. I had been a "One Date Charlie" for a couple of months and truly needed a break...or so I thought. I was definitely not looking for love that night.

My giant duffle bag of clean laundry, and me with my swollen eyes and red nose, from allergies to my parents' cat, all caught the 8:34 p.m. Long Island Railroad train home.

Jack was happy and feeling relieved having ended a recent relationship, and certainly wasn't looking for love that night.

He visited his father every Sunday, and his dad had just moved to Huntington six weeks prior. They always looked forward to ending their day with a nice dinner out.

His plan was to catch the 7:30 p.m. train back to the city.

Jack was getting ready to pay the check when the waitress said, "This is a prix fixe dinner; you still have dessert and coffee."

What to do?

In a life-changing decision, Jack and his dad decided to

enjoy the dessert, coffee, and company, and he would now take the 8:34 train instead.

Across the aisle and facing me sat Jack.

I was reading a section of the Sunday *New York Times*. Jack casually asked me what I was looking for in the paper. This led to an interesting conversation that lasted the rest of the ride back, which was only ten minutes.

As we were approaching Penn Station, Jack quickly asked if we could go out for a drink or a bite to eat...sometime. I didn't catch the last couple of words, and thought he was being so forward asking me out for that very night. I really just wanted to get home and soak my itchy eyes, but something powerful inside me told me to say yes.

I can't believe that I agreed... "But I've got these laundry bags."

Jack helped me home. We went out for dessert, his second of the night. We have never stopped talking or had a day apart since.

We just celebrated our silver wedding anniversary. Twenty-five incredible years, due to a change in train times!

It's quite amazing how we can wake up in the morning and have no idea how drastically life can change by the end of the evening.

We never really know where a love connection can pop up.

Sometimes just going against your own grain can open up an opportunity that takes your life in the most unexpected direction.

32

THE DINER
Sheila & Al

I WANTED TO MEET THE love of my life, for the rest of my life!

At sixty-eight, divorced and living in New York City, I was dating a great deal through all the traditional ways. I was discouraged and disappointed when they didn't work out.

I'm a terrific woman.... Where was my terrific man?

Al, seventy-five, was widowed for less than a year, after being married for fifty years.

One Sunday morning, Al went for breakfast at the Scarsdale Diner in a suburb of New York City.

Ellie, Sheila's friend, was there with her niece. Ellen spotted Al, who was wearing his alma mater (Lehigh) sweatshirt. It was the same university she attended, and she went to his table to say hello—a pivotal moment.

Ellie joined the conversation. After a few moments of chatting, she thought Al was a great guy and wasn't letting this opportunity go. It was a lightbulb moment!

She asked Al if he was single. She had a friend to introduce him to.

Al asked where the friend lived, and when she responded Manhattan, he quickly let her know that Sheila was geographically undesirable.

He quipped, "Elizabeth Taylor asked me out, but I said no because she lived in the city."

Ellie said, "Go once, Al, just go once."

He went. The rest, as they say, is history.

We were married ten months later, and for the past fourteen years have continued to enjoy life together in Florida.

Sheila says, "Let everyone you know that you are looking for love. You never know when it will find you!"

33
My Last First Date
Randee & Alan

My story does not begin with how I met the love of my life.

It begins with two broken marriages and a horrific three-year relationship that didn't end well.

It took me to this point in my life to be committed to making the right choices about men.

I can definitely say that I was a slow learner, naïve, and immature in choosing the men in my life.

So my story begins with breaking away from the awful relationship with a man I initially thought was good but, truth be told, was not good at all.

I put myself into therapy not only to break away but to love myself again.

I was so broken down that the last thing I wanted to do was date.

I had a lot of self-love and self-care work to do to build myself back up.

I knew I had a lot to give and wanted to find that special man who would give to me also. When I felt ready to date, I did so with a much better sense of self.

After many disappointing dates, life changed on November 19, 2020. I had another first date.

I walked into the restaurant and saw him sitting at the table waiting for me.

He looked up and he smiled. As we sat across from each other, we looked into each other's eyes, and he placed his hands across the table palms up. I reached forward and put my hands in his.

We didn't say anything to each other in those first few moments ... just continued to smile at each other. It was a moment in time I will never forget.

We began to talk and share about our lives. A man who listened, opened up, and had depth. I struck gold!

At one point, I remember him leaning over the table to kiss me so sweetly. It was all so incredible.

He drove me home and invited me to his aunt's house for Thanksgiving.

I accepted, and our time together has been nothing short of miraculous!

On November 19, 2021, there were fireworks in the street as we celebrated the first anniversary of our life-changing first date.

Little did I know that only a year ago I would find the "love of my life."

Alan is my best friend, my confidant, my teacher, my partner. I love the present and I can't wait to see what the future brings.

I am very proud to say he is my person, and I am his.

My advice...never, never, never give up! All that I went through in the past brought me to my love and was worth every tear. And it can happen for you too.

34
GEOGRAPHICALLY UNDESIRABLE
Robert & Susan

DIVORCED AND ON MY OWN for several years, I was ready to try again.

New York Magazine Personals was the Match.com of the era so I placed an ad.

Many women responded and I culled the list to twelve strong possibilities.

At the very same time, my dad was ill and my mom his caretaker. She was hospitalized and needed a surgical procedure, so I came to stay with Dad.

He went to sleep at 8 p.m. and slept through the night. I was bored (no cable TV) and fidgety but free to go out for a few hours.

My parents lived in Queens, and I was living in New Jersey, which was at least a forty-five-minute drive.

Then I remembered that there was actually one on my list of twelve dating prospects who lived in Queens—Susan.

I called her and we had an immediate and fun conversation.

I checked on my dad and went to meet her at a diner halfway between our locations.

I felt a real connection immediately. But she lived in Queens and I was only going to be at my parents' home for two more nights! Did I even want to start a relationship with someone in another state?

We made the best of it. We met both nights, going to the San Genaro Street festival and to a Chinese restaurant in Flushing.

Yes, she was geographically undesirable, but I knew that she was very special. I liked her. A lot.

What should I do? I was going to continue to date her and let this play out.

Then something unbelievable occurred that totally changed the location issue for both of us.

A few weeks after our powerful and memorable dates, on one of our lengthy phone conversations, we realized that we hadn't even begun to touch upon our childhoods.

I began. I talked about my fond memories of going to a small summer camp near the Catskill Mountains.

Sue asked me lots of questions. The name of the camp and what year I was there.

She asked if there was color war there and when I said yes, "I was on the Orange team," she burst out in song.

"Fight men of Orange, never more to yield."

How could she know this? Impossible!

This was the song from 1958. My camp song! I was confused, but I sang along.

We knew this was bigger than both of us when she proceeded to tell me that she was there the very same year. At the same small camp. She was twelve and I was fourteen. I cherished my summers there, so it was extremely bonding.

Sue cleverly had T-shirts made for us with the camp's name on the front and staff printed on the back.

We wore our shirts when we visited the camp together and had fun sharing our memories along the drive up.

How could I ever resist this woman? This was meant to be!

Thirty-five years later, we share a wonderful life with three kids (two are hers, one is mine), six grandchildren, and three granddogs.

We did not let two bridges, the Cross-Bronx Expressway, and full-time jobs derail our new romance.

The distance between us became insignificant and so worth the effort.

The memory of our first meeting is still strong. It was so unexpected and so empowering.

Connections are found at the most inopportune times and in the most unusual settings. This was ours.

My advice is to take advantage of opportunities that present themselves. Don't be afraid to step outside your comfort zone.

" Sometimes what you're looking for comes when you're not looking at all. "

~Fiona Childs

A Happy Twist of Fate
Nikki & Leonard

WHEN I WAS ABOUT TO turn fifty, my mother told me that this would be one of the most wonderful times of my life.

She said it but truly had no idea if it would come true and neither did I. However, that statement did give me hope, which I needed.

It was to be a year of many changes and passages: closing my store, getting divorced after an unhappy marriage, my son moving out on his own, me moving to New York City with no job and only $5,000 to my name.

I was excited to begin anew. I was a city girl and happy to be back.

My best friend gave me a subscription to *New York Magazine*, and in a tiny box in the back of the magazine was an ad for The Art Lover's League.

I thought I would look into joining, not to meet men but, I hoped, to make new friends, see theater, museums, etc.

The Art Lover's League turned out to be an old-fashioned matchmaker run by a lovely mature lady in New England. She said she was pretty good at putting people together; in fact, had already matched eight couples! (A happy twist of fate.)

Why not be adventurous? I said to myself. Go for it.

I had my doubts, but she convinced me to give it a try. All of this was done with a two-page questionnaire.

A few weeks later I received paragraphs from three men... two sounded promising.

After an interesting, fun-filled, and very long conversation with the second man, Leonard, we made plans to meet for a drink.

That one drink turned into a three-hour dinner. I found myself instantly attracted to his humor and totally enchanted with this man.

There was just something about him. I loved being in his company and we found that we had a great deal in common.

That night I knew that I met the man of my dreams.

We've been together for twenty years. We just got married after having to postpone the wedding twice because of COVID.

He promised that he would make me laugh every day... and he has kept his promise!

My advice is to focus on you and take care of you, follow the path of what you love. You are the most important person. If you do that it will all fall into place.

By innocently answering that ad for the Art Lover's League, my life changed forever.

I never would have thought that at fifty, it would happen in such a serendipitous way.

If it happened for me, it could happen for you!

36

Fly Me To The Moon
Susan & Bruce

I HAD ENDED AN EXCITING, combined dance and love relationship earlier in 2014.

I loved being around men—interesting ones, of course. I was looking for funny, fun, intellectual, and sincere.

As I matured, I realized that we are in a far better position to make conscious choices regarding relationships.

All the "not so good" relationships are simply great learning experiences that prepare you for the right one.

I left my marriage in 2002 and it was final in February 2004. I met Bruce in 2014. Wow! Ten years.

I was never counting the days. I never consider my age as a negative and never thought younger women were a threat.

I was sixty-three-years-old when Bruce and I met. I have always felt all things are possible.

I feel that subconsciously I was always looking for love. I think we all are. We are wired that way.

My dance partner and I had ended our relationship on friendly terms about six months earlier.

I was not really taking a break. I was open to what presented itself.

I was not an online dating kind of girl—that seemed so unnatural to me.

My heart was always open to dating. I was never anxious about finding the right partner at any specific time.

Then one day the universe delivered a most interesting man in my life, in a very unusual way.

One evening after a yoga class I walked into Trader Joe's in Encinitas, California, looking for fruit, certainly not romance. It was the first Thursday of June. I remember it well.

As I approached the banana stand this bloke walked up and began to sing "Fly Me to the Moon"—to me.

I was astonished because I had started doing talent management and I had just signed a contract with a crooner.

Music was so much a part of my life primarily because it is the music that drives the dance, and dancing was my love.

Bruce, who was sixty-two and a free spirit, had been divorced for several years and he was frolicking about everywhere he went.

When I heard his voice, I thought, He's really got something here. I was fascinated.

Bruce and I first had coffee together and then started going to jazz clubs in town, where he would sing.

We also would go to a club in La Jolla, California, where we danced the night away.

It wasn't love at first sight. I wasn't really a gal who went for love too quickly, although I was intrigued with Bruce and his life as a fashion photographer in New York.

He was bright as well as a great storyteller, combined with a marvelous sense of humor.

It wasn't until I returned in the fall from New York, where I spent my birthday wish of dancing at the Rainbow Room with my dance partner from Washington DC, that I really connected with Bruce.

We have been together a little over seven years, and in the fall of 2017, we moved to Cuenca, Ecuador.

We are linked together on several levels and are delightfully happy.

My meeting Bruce was definitely unexpected. So my advice is, even if you go shopping for bananas, always keep your heart and eyes open. You may wind up with a fabulous man in your life!

Young Love
Bev & Jeff

Most people have a high school sweetheart, including me. We dated from eleventh grade through our early twenties, but just couldn't seem to get it right.

The timing was always off for one of us to really commit. We ended up going our separate ways. Me into New York City, and Jeff to starting his own business in New Jersey.

I got married. Jeff got married.

And although from time to time I would think about Jeff and what he was up to, our paths did not cross again.

Until we both decided separately to go to our high school reunion about thirty years ago.

I went with my then husband and Jeff came with his wife. We danced, we talked, we flirted a bit, and then went our separate ways.

About nine years later, I went to a Joni Mitchell concert. Jeff and I had gone to see her when we were dating in the mid-1980s.

It made me think of him again. So I wrote him a note, telling him about the concert and asking how he was doing.

I sent it to the only address that I had, which was a post office box for his business, not expecting to hear back from him. About a month later, I got a voicemail at work—from Jeff.

I was in the process of separating from my husband at the time.

I later found out Jeff had lost his wife several years earlier.

We planned to meet for dinner in New Jersey a few months later. I will never forget walking up to the restaurant and seeing him there waiting for me out front.

I was shaking, scared, excited, anticipating I don't know what.

We sat and talked for hours. Neither of us could really eat.

After dinner we walked through town and went to sit on a park bench.

I knew that if we were going to kiss, I would have to be the one to make that happen. We kissed. That was it.

We both knew that our lives were about to change forever and that we would have to move mountains to make it happen.

But we also knew that we could and would do whatever it took to be together, to blend our families because this time the time was right.

We were both equally committed. We got married about a year and a half later and will be married twenty years this coming June.

This is a love story that needed to happen. To this day I am still amazed that we are together as a couple, as a family.

We have had great tragedy and great joy in this journey. But there is no one I'd rather share this life with than Jeff.

There are happy endings and new beginnings if you can see beyond the obstacles. It's so much easier to say, "No, I can't do this...it's too hard...it's impossible." It's much harder to shut your eyes, trust your heart, and say "Yes, let's make this happen."

38

THE ONE THAT ALMOST GOT AWAY
Liz and Daryl

FOUR YEARS AGO, I WAS active in the miserable world of online dating. I matched with a man whom I texted with briefly and spoke on the phone with once.

I was, however, starting to date someone else at the same time. I basically blew off this lovely man whom I briefly spoke to.

Four years passed and the relationship I had been in ended leaving me in painful shattered pieces, feeling as empty as I'd ever felt. The situation was just awful, and I thought I'd never even consider dating, ever.

One evening at a work gathering, my dear friend Sam strongly suggested that I give it another try.

As nervous as I was, I knew nobody was dropping from the heavens for me, so I went online yet again.

I giggled when I saw the same man, Daryl, from four years ago.

I took a chance and swiped right. The words flashed across the screen: It's a Match!

We started texting with only me knowing that we had spoken in the past. I kind of figured he didn't remember. He asked if he could call me, and I said yes.

When the phone rang, his name appeared because I already had his number in my phone.

When I answered he asked if we had spoken before. I explained what had happened and we laughed over it. One week later we decided to meet in person. After a beautiful evening, we decided to see one another the following week.

We were both careful, but we also knew that we enjoyed each other's company. We took it slowly until a couple of months later when the ball dropped on January 1. He told me that he loved me! I knew that I loved him too.

Soon after, he was offered a job opportunity in Chicago, where his family lives, but he turned it down to stay with me in New York.

It was a defining moment in our relationship. It was a huge risk to take but we knew we didn't want to be that far apart.

Months went by and we continued to grow deeper in love. We were creating wonderful memories together and would often visit a quaint little town called New Hope, Pennsylvania.

We absolutely love it there. We popped into an adorable little jewelry and gift shop and saw an absolutely beautiful ring, so beautiful that I couldn't stop thinking about it when we got home.

At that point we had discussed the idea of marriage and living together on Long Island where I live. He eventually moved in.

After settling in for a couple of weeks, we drove to pick up a very dear friend from the airport. This was a friend whom I hadn't seen in over five years.

When we got home, we saw my parents there and naturally figured they were there to surprise my friend, as they knew her as a child.

They exchanged hugs and we were all gathered around talking. My mom pulled me aside to tell me that she needed to talk to me. Darryl followed, although I didn't see him.

And that's when he asked me to marry him!

I was honestly so shocked that I was speechless.

My friend had no idea that this was coming so all I could hear were her screams.

She had been there for me during all my past romantic ups and downs, so it was very special for her to witness this incredible moment.

He reached into his pocket to pull out the exact ring that I fell in love with from New Hope. Even the name fits—New Hope!

I was at my lowest point when this incredible man came into my life. I shudder to think that he almost got away.

Don't ever give up finding your diamond. Keep your heart open until you find someone whose imperfections are perfect for you!

THE BACHELOR
Joy & MS

WHAT IF? I ACTUALLY DID meet the next love of my life. What if? It was at a time that was least expected.

I had always carried fate in my back pocket. I believed that if you wanted something bad enough, thought about it enough, and kept positive intentions with a positive attitude—fate would step in.

I was feeling pretty darn good about myself. Throughout the years I had taken self-care seriously, and I have to say both my inner and outer selves were in great shape. I was ready for my next great long-term loving relationship.

I had been married and divorced, with grown children and grandchildren and a full life. Yet, there I was hoping that fate was going to step in and introduce me to my waiting future! But most definitely, not that night.

It did step in, disguised as coincidence.

I arranged to meet with the owner of a local restaurant to propose an idea I had for an event, and I had a good friend meeting me there for dinner.

I was a little early. I sat at the bar to wait for my friend and began reviewing details for the event with the owner. He and I finished up when I received a text saying my friend had canceled out on our dinner.

I was alone at the bar finishing my wine when a woman I knew walked out of a side door that led to a private room. She stopped at the bar. Hellos were exchanged and she told me she was holding a meeting that night for an upcoming bachelor auction. It was a fundraiser for a children's charity.

I decided to have a bite to eat at the bar. Around ten o'clock, the charity meeting was breaking up and the bachelors were streaming out of the private room.

One of them, MS, stopped in his tracks and came right over to me. He said that we had previously met but could not remember where or when. We tried to figure it out, had some laughs about it, and he finally realized that it was from a dating site I was on some months ago for a thirty-day trial, which I chose to discontinue.

Not only did he respond to my information, but he kept my photo on his computer screen, so of course I was very familiar to him that evening. I told him how odd that was because I had been off the site for months.

Unbeknownst to me they had kept my photo and bio on the site.

He wrote to me and often wondered why I hadn't replied back.

Sparks were already flying between us.

If my friend had made it to dinner, we would have been sitting at a table in the restaurant and missed all the action and especially MS, who came out of that bar door an hour later.

And here we were sitting in a restaurant that neither of us had ever been to, this along with the coincidence of the dating site and my friend not meeting me for dinner. Coincidence? I don't think so!

Coincidence removed her disguise and fate stepped in. We fell in love and had an amazing four years of love, laughter, and delight. It was not a forever romance. We both grew personally from the relationship and remain friends.

My advice. Life is a mysterious adventure filled with the unexpected. Don't give up your dreams. And remember that fate has many disguises and has a habit of finding you when least expected.

"Once in a while, right in the middle of ordinary life, love gives us a fairy tale.

~Unknown

40

HAPPY BIRTHDAY, WRONG NUMBER
Zoë & Wil

BEFORE I MET Wil, I was working on myself, and I was feeling pretty good about it.

I wasn't focusing on finding a relationship. I only had one serious relationship in the past and it ultimately didn't work out.

After a while I had gotten used to being single and I was fine with it, which is typically when people walk into your life. Right when everything is in the sweet spot, and you never see them coming.

That's exactly what happened with Wil.

We had a nonromantic past, which is why I just never thought we would have a love relationship, let alone the person I would spend the rest of my life with.

We met at the French Woods Festival, a vibrant performing arts camp filled with the most talented kids you could imagine. He was very popular around the camp, as his mother worked there, and all of his siblings attended the camp as well.

I never once thought of him as more than a cute, cool, and popular guy from my camp. Why would he be interested in me?

That day began like any other when it happened. It was totally out of the blue, with a life-changing text message from him wishing me a happy birthday.

But it wasn't my birthday!

There was, in fact, another Zoë with a birthday on that date and he thought it was me.

It felt so funny that it sparked a conversation, and then we just never stopped. A little mistake like that turned out to be the best thing that ever happened to me.

Wil fit into my life so well and he supported me in all the ways I needed and wanted to be supported.

Every relationship has its ups and downs, and we worked through those difficult moments as a team. That's why I'm excited to continue building a life with someone whom I love as a friend and as a partner.

We are engaged now, planning our wedding, and looking forward to our marriage that all began with a wrong number. This was truly meant to be.

Keep holding on to your dreams while you are living your life. That's the best advice I can give. Don't put too much focus on finding the one since chance encounters show up when you least expect them to.

Fall in love with someone who is your best friend with whom you can have fun doing absolutely anything and nothing. One who supports you and loves you for you!

41
FAMOUS LAST WORDS
Gina & Anthony

I AM NEVER GOING TO get married again is what I said to all who listened after my dismal marriage came to an end.

Since I knew that I was never going to get married again, I created a wonderful life for myself with an incredible support system. I was more than okay living alone.

There were more nights than not that I was happy to get cozy with a book and a glass of wine. I enjoyed going out with friends, had some fine romances, and played tennis as much as I could.

I was truly comfortable being on my own. My relationship with myself was deepening. I was falling in love with me. I felt nourished.

I was privy to the inner goings-on in a few of my friends' marriages and found that for the most part, the grass was not greener.

Except for the occasional lonely days and nights.

They were hard ones. On those days, I longed for a partner to comfort me when work was stressful. I would have loved a strong shoulder to lean my head on when my parents were sick. Holidays and weddings were especially difficult.

And then—three years, four months, two weeks and three days ago—something extraordinary happened!

It was a day like most others. I went off to work, to a job I love, and later went to visit my very ill dad, in the hospital. He had been alone in a double room until that fateful day.

A man was moved into his room after his surgery. His son came to be with him, and we exchanged pleasantries. I was extremely attracted to the tender way he spoke to his father and how he cared for him. Be still my heart.

My dad was not doing well, and I was in the family lounge feeling very teary, when along came the son of the roommate. He came right over to me as he heard me crying softly.

Anthony asked if he could get me coffee or anything else. Then he just sat next to me and let me feel my feelings.

We barely spoke but it was comforting. I was so appreciative and let him know. Now this was the kind of a man whose shoulder I would love to have put my head on.

His father was released the next day. I never saw him again.

Until—months later, a friend invited me to her tennis club in Englewood, New Jersey on a Saturday morning. After playing, we went to get a cold drink at the cafe.

Walking toward me was someone who looked very familiar. He had a big smile and said, "Do you remember me?"

Yes, it was the son! Did I remember him? You bet.

Anthony told me that he often thought about me. He wondered how my dad was doing and how I was coping.

I neglected to tell him how often I thought about that chance encounter until our wedding day.

My lonely nights are no more. I truly was ready for a deep connection. I didn't even realize how much I wanted a special love in my life. I was mature enough to know how to communicate effectively and how to ask for what I needed.

I now have a partner with a huge heart who only wants to help make my life easier. I do the same for him.

My advice is to create the very best life you can. Learn everything you can about yourself. Keep growing so that when a serendipitous encounter happens you are prepared and ready to love and be loved. Even when you had very powerfully said never again!

42
THE MATZO BALL
Julia & Howard

MY STORY IS NOT UNLIKE many other single women. If there was an unavailable man around, I somehow found him. I was like a magnet, attracting men who didn't want what I wanted.

What went along with dating the unavailables came many disappointments, canceled plans, holidays alone, and many other frustrations.

There were many positives as well but when the disappointments outweighed them, I sought out help and finally had the courage to end it. Brava to me.

I did catch myself thinking that there may not be anyone else to make me smile again. I often asked myself if there was anyone who would ever capture my heart?

I proved to myself that I could be alone, which felt very powerful, but just because I was ready to find love for myself didn't mean that it was going to show up so easily.

At forty-eight, life otherwise was terrific. I had great friends and a great job. All that was missing was a romantic available partner. I had an overflow of love to give to a deserving man.

What I didn't know was that my friend's adult daughter had recently asked her if she knew anyone for her soon-to-be father-in-law, Howard, to meet.

He was recently divorced, and after taking time to sort

it all out, was ready to date. My friend immediately said my name and, unbeknownst to me, they made plans for a future meeting.

Before this meeting ever happened, I was encouraged to go to a dance on Christmas Eve for Jewish people called the Matzo Ball.

I reluctantly went as it was not my thing.

I pushed myself to go because this was the new me. I was open to all possibilities. I wanted to be more of a yes-to-life person, especially my dating life.

When I arrived to give my name and get my entrance ticket, the very first person I saw sitting at the check-in desk was my friend's daughter.

And Howard was there too! It was his very first outing ever as a single man.

She lit up when she saw me and said, "I have someone for you to meet." She found Howard and introduced us.

He asked me to dance. We clicked immediately and we danced the night away.

Howard asked me out for New Year's Eve, which was the next week.

It was the beginning of a new year and a new romantic life. I was smiling again, full of love both giving and receiving.

And yes, we have been married for over twenty years.

My advice to women is to be a yes to all possibilities, even if it seems to be out of your comfort zone. Just say yes.

Life can change on a dime. Remember, I didn't know Howard when I woke up that morning. I didn't want to go to that party. It can happen for you too!

43

DON'T QUIT BEFORE THE MIRACLE
Jill & Don

AFTER A SIX-YEAR NIGHTMARE of a relationship, I woke up at thirty-six-years-old, and told my mom, "If I'm still single at forty-years-old, do not have a party for me."

If there was one thing I knew in life, it was that I wanted to get married and have children.

Well, that fateful summer, my mom was having her second wedding and at that black-tie affair, when Mom threw her bouquet, I went after it like it was the Hope Diamond.

She'd accidentally thrown it way off to the side, and let me tell you something—I ran in my long gown and high heels and I threw myself on top of that doomed beautiful bouquet, crushing it between my stomach and the highly polished dance floor.

I wanted it badly, so I guess that was the way I told the universe.

My lucky number is seventeen, my birthdate. Exactly seventeen days later, and within only a short time after declaring to my mother, therefore the universe, that I would refuse to celebrate forty if I were still single, I met the one!

I had been getting my life back together after that awful six years that almost tore my life down.

I had started a new job as national sales manager and was at my very first trade show representing the company in

Atlanta.

That first day, another vendor, a man, made eye contact with me from across the room. He soon left his post and came over to introduce himself.

He was friendly, welcoming, and playful and that made me feel so much better because it was my first time as a manager and I was feeling nervous, not knowing anyone at all.

I sensed the flirtation. Another vendor gal I'd met that day and I became like giddy schoolgirls, curious about him.

Well, we went to dinner together the following night and he was just the best. I knew he was smitten with me, and he became my hero in so many ways.

Don instantly and easily became a trusted friend. I could ask him any questions about this business without worrying that it made me look unqualified.

I started to look forward to seeing him at each town that followed. Maybe I was a bit smitten with him too, but I didn't quite admit it to myself—yet.

In Chicago, we went to Navy Pier one evening and he asked to hold my hand. When you know, girls, you just know. And I knew. This was real.

So, that night, I relaxed a little more. We linked arms. I let my guard down and we talked and laughed for hours.

Between shows, we were emailing each other and getting closer.

By Boston, we'd fallen in love. It was everything two people could hope for.

He went back home and sent me a CD of songs he had been listening to that made him think of me. When I listened to it, I cried my eyes out. I knew he was the one!

He moved in with me and commuted one hundred miles each way, each day, for months and months just to be with me.

When that Atlanta show came around again, exactly one year to the day we met, standing in the same spot of the showroom where we originally locked eyes, while business was going on around us, he proposed!

We married and immediately began our family. I often say it would've been a crime had Don not had children.

Our incredible daughters are now fifteen and thirteen, and Don and I have been together for eighteen years.

It was all meant to be. Don't quit five minutes, or seventeen days, before the miracle. And tell the universe what you want. Go after it. Crush those bouquets!

44

APARTMENT HUNTING
Connie & Jim

MEMORIAL DAY IN 1978 CERTAINLY was memorable for me. That date, May 25, changed my life.

I had been living in California for several years after being raised in Springfield, Massachusetts. I wanted to get a fresh start, and I intrinsically knew that I had to live in New York City. It was a calling, as if I knew my life would flourish if I moved there.

I called a dear friend. Could I crash on her couch until I found a job? Her generous yes was authentic and a lifeline.

I loved everything about where she lived. It was in a charming Upper West Side neighborhood, mainly brownstones with beautiful architecture from the early 1920s.

I immediately found a position at JC Penney working in corporate communications. This position seemed promising since I had worked as a producer in public television at KGO in San Francisco.

A real job in a major company in the best city in the world. This meant that I could afford to get my own apartment.

On the weekends for exercise, I jogged around the neighborhood and knew that this was where I wanted to live. It felt so right. I was in my element.

I got the real estate section of *The New York Times*, the place to go for the best Manhattan apartments. I began looking around on the block I picked as the one.

It was West 105th Street between West End and Riverside, a landmark street with Beaux Arts limestone townhouses with black wrought iron terraces—a slice of Paris in New York. I was advised to be strong and assertive in my search since there was such a demand for apartments.

Never did I think that my romantic life would change on that day to the degree that it did. I still get the chills thinking of how it all happened when I least expected it.

As I strolled down 105th Street, I was surprised to see a very attractive man sitting on the top stoop of his brownstone where he had an apartment. I told him of my plight to find an apartment and asked if he knew of any available units in the neighborhood.

We had an instant connection, an easy and wonderful conversation. We both felt it. He said he knew some supers in the neighborhood and would be happy to float some inquiries.

We exchanged numbers, ostensibly to work on the apartment search, but I think both of us also simply wanted to find a way to stay in touch.

He asked me if I wanted to see his apartment. He had just moved in that morning and was clearly very excited about it. Knowing from our conversation that he was a school counselor made me feel safe. Up I went.

The conversation kept flowing and the connection was so strong that I felt excited to have a new friend. This was a real quality man.

Later the next week, Jim asked me if I would like to go to a street fair with him and his young daughter. We had a great day, and she and I bonded over dinner.

I desperately wanted an apartment and yet instead, the universe sent me a fabulous, kind, intelligent, interesting man.

My past relationships had been disastrous. I made poor choices and promised myself that I would do everything in my power to stop attracting or being attracted to the same type of man.

Jim was just the opposite of everyone else that I had ever

dated. Before meeting Jim, I had told myself that I would stop looking for my next partner and first get comfortable with myself.

Jim later told me that before he came out to the stoop, he turned on the water to take a shower and at the last minute changed his mind and decided to sit outside instead.

Fate had stepped in. Our unexpected, unusual meeting was serendipitous. It was meant to be.

I went from moving to Manhattan to moving in with my man!

I am happy to say that my husband and I have been together for the past forty-three years.

My advice? Well, it's a bit complex but here goes. Some might say we both had good luck, and to an extent that is true. Contingency always plays a role in life's events, but readiness and intentionality are also part of the formula.

What if Jim had jumped into the shower that morning? Would we have ever met?

I had been doing some internal work on myself, to be more mindful and selective in entering relationships.

I had opened myself up not only to the universe of the possible but to the type of man who might present qualities that were more nurturing and supportive to my needs.

Some say that good luck happens when opportunity meets being ready and mindful.

So, be open, be sensible, and take a risk that is informed by spirituality and common sense!

" Sometimes you fall in love with the most unexpected person at the most unexpected time. "

~Unknown

THE COACH
Jennifer & Dan

I WAS MARRIED FOR TEN years. We met when I was only twenty-three; he was ten years my senior. While our marriage did not last, I can't say I regret it since we have three beautiful children.

I took the role of stay-at-home mom after we had our oldest in 2002. All I ever wanted to be since I was a little girl was a mom, so I absolutely loved it.

I found myself with more time on my hands when our children entered school. It was then that I realized just how much my husband and I had grown apart. We were more like roommates, living very separate lives. It was not a partnership and not a happy or healthy marriage.

One day it hit me, I wanted my children to grow up seeing love, seeing what a healthy and loving relationship looked like, and this was not a good example for them, so I filed for divorce.

It was absolutely the hardest, most emotional experience I've ever had. I remember thinking that it would be easier since so many marriages end in divorce, but I was very wrong.

I needed a manual, but since I didn't find exactly what worked for me, I had to figure it out on my own.

I will be forever grateful for the support I had from family and friends and forever proud that I had the strength to do something so scary.

After my divorce I would often spend my weekends driving myself to New York City from Connecticut and running races with the NY Runners Club. Running kept me active and it was something I did just for me. It's been a form of therapy.

I was really learning a lot about myself and becoming comfortable on my own and within myself.

On April 14, 2013, I was heading back from NYC after running the *More Magazine* women's half marathon. It was a beautiful day. I was feeling great, but I had a time restraint that day.

My oldest son had his first baseball practice of the season that early afternoon. He had been drafted as a nine-year-old to the ten-year-old all-star team. I am a big-time sports mom, so I make it my mission to make sure they get to practices and games on time.

So there I was, trying to run a fast race so I could jump into the car and drive back to Connecticut to pick him up at home and head to the field.

I definitely didn't want to be the reason he didn't have a positive first impression from the coach, so we rushed. I hadn't even taken off my running shoes and probably even still had my running bib on. I wasn't exactly looking, or smelling, my best.

I wanted to say hello to the new coach, Michael, and introduce myself. My plan was to say, "Hi, my name is Jenn— this is my son. I'm so sorry we're just getting here," and then leave. But he had this calming tone to him and after he introduced himself, he said no worries, and then told us a bit about the team.

From then on, he was so helpful with offering rides to practices when I was stuck and just checking in with us, especially since my son was one of the younger ones on the team and was very shy.

We started texting a bit, kind of flirty, and when the season came to an end I wondered if we'd see one another again.

He asked me out on a date after the last game. That date

led to many, many more and ultimately to our wedding!

My oldest son walked me down the aisle in 2016. My middle son carried our rings, and my daughter was our flower girl.

I am most grateful that my children had the experience of seeing their mom happy and witnessing a loving relationship.

I encourage anyone who finds themself in a position like I did, alone and maybe a bit lost, unsure when, where, and if they will ever be in another relationship, to be open, don't rush it, and breathe deeply.

If I had just turned around to run back to my car to head home to finally shower, I might have missed out. You never know what, or who, might be around the corner.

It may be super unexpected, and they may not be who you thought they would be or what they would look like. But they just might be your other half.

46

THE BUTTERFLY ON MY SHOULDER

Margaret & Alex

AT AGE FORTY-FOUR, I had followed the expected life path of schooling, marriage, children, and middle-age exercising, yet I was still painfully unhappy.

I found myself feeling guilty about being unhappy. Should I just accept the adage that people can die at forty-five but are not buried until eighty-five?

My jobs became yet another exercise to not think about my guilt because I was so unhappy, even though society and my family thought I had it all.

I mustered the self-survival courage to separate from my unfulfilling relationship after my children were in college. I needed to laugh, to breathe, to hope, and to love myself again.

After losing a dream job due to corporate restructuring, I walked into a start-up company interview with the founder.

Our immediate connection through our initial eye contact only initiated the soon-to-follow exciting dialogue of laughter, respect, and curiosity.

As I walked out of the interview, I felt I had just met someone unlike anyone I had ever met before. Of course, I dispatched my friends to work, googling and researching him so I could find something wrong. I didn't.

After the interview I went home and called the headhunter to say that I would take the job only to find out that it was already being offered to me.

It was meant to be.

Our professional relationship was platonic and yet exciting. We worked closely together, but never an awkward pause or inappropriate move.

This went on for months. We traveled a great deal to visit with our many franchisees. Alex, ever the gentleman, made separate room reservations in any hotel in which we were to stay.

My muses intervened when we arrived in a town where the National Poodle Convention was being held.

Through no fault of ours, except muse interference, there was only one room left in the inn. We drove to four other hotels trying to find two rooms available.

Upon returning to hotel number one, we decided I would take the bed and he would take the couch. Suffice it to say, the following morning our romantic relationship had begun, and poodles are still our favorite dog.

Our relationship has always had elements of adventure, mutual respect, and an ability to accept each other's personalities as they are.

We never try to change each other but rather to present a united front while lending unconditional support to each other.

Although there have been challenging times during our twenty-five-year marriage, where this has been tested, our relationship is simply easy.

I no longer have to rethink what I am going to say. I don't fear criticism or disagreement. It is simply like an old sweater that just feels warm and comfortable.

I found my best friend and life partner during a time of my life when I thought I had been forgotten.

The memories of my life are mostly recalled in black and white. The recollection of finally meeting my long-awaited, and almost giving up hope of ever finding my soul mate, is recalled in a rainbow of colors and fireworks.

I guess finding love is like chasing a butterfly in an open field. If we try too hard to catch it, it evades us.

However, when we are at peace with ourselves, the butterfly will land on our shoulders when we least expect it.

47

SERENDIPITY WORKING ITS MAGIC
Ana & Michael

BY THE END OF 2005, I had concluded that I was alone in this world, without a special someone. Countless, dateless Friday nights offset by flaky, boring dates.

I had spent most of this year thinking about my future. Should I remain in California or return home to San Antonio, Texas? My dad was diagnosed with stage four cancer. The news broke my heart. I adored my father.

I was flying to Texas almost every month throughout 2005 to spend time with my family. I was feeling very alone and helpless in California. On top of everything, my fortieth birthday was fast approaching.

I was heading back to Los Angeles after spending the holidays with family in Texas. The rarity about that night was that my brother Alex was late, which was totally out of character for him. We were in rush hour traffic, and I was crossing my fingers that I would not miss the flight.

I was the last passenger to arrive at Southwest gate six. Had I arrived on time, this story probably wouldn't be written.

As it turned out, I was not going to hold my status as the last passenger in line. I felt someone tap me on the shoulder and say hello. I turned, and because I am only five feet tall, I was staring at a striped shirt! And a voice from above said, "Up here—I'm a little taller than you." At over six feet he was, in fact, a foot taller than me.

He introduced himself and told me that he was currently living in Ontario, California. He was in San Antonio for a one-day real estate auction. I found Michael very entertaining in his conversation, and actually quite handsome.

We were separated as we boarded, and I found a seat toward the back. I watched Michael board as he found a seat toward the front.

As soon as the seatbelt sign went off Michael stood up, turned toward the back, and called my name. I was mortified.

When I looked up, he was motioning for me to come sit with him, yelling what a nice guy he was and worth getting to know.

By now the other passengers were encouraging me to go sit with him, so I did. They all clapped.

We spent the next two hours talking about our lives. He was funny and spontaneous and in possession of the most intense blue eyes.

We parted ways in Phoenix, as he headed off to catch his connecting flight to Ontario, California. I remained on the plane on my way to LAX. We had exchanged cards and I wondered as we descended into Los Angeles if I would hear from him.

The next morning as I was driving to work along Pacific Coast Highway, I kept thinking about Michael and how he stood up in the plane and searched me out. I loved his spontaneity. As I pulled into my parking space, the phone rang but with no identification.

The billowing voice I heard was Michael's. "Hi, are you available for dinner?" I was a yes.

We spent the next few weeks inseparable and we're still together.

Our four-year courtship was a whirlwind of adventure and happiness. We were married in Carmel, California.

Our son Dylan is now fourteen and a perfect combination of the two of us. Our home in San Antonio is filled with love and good times.

They say only two percent of the population meet at an airport. I like to think it was serendipity working its magic.

Anything is possible—I really do believe that. Don't ever forget that, even on the darkest of days.

48

GUESS WHO CAME TO DINNER?
Nora & Tom

I RETURNED HOME FOR MY sophomore year of college after spending my second consecutive summer in Southern California. I was depressed. I had fallen in love with the West Coast and didn't want to be anywhere else, especially not back on Long Island.

Shortly thereafter I got very ill with pneumonia and had to drop out of classes. Not walking pneumonia, but in bed, lifeless, a very serious type of pneumonia, and looking sickly.

At about the two-week mark, with cabin fever setting in, my sister took pity on me and took me on a drive just to get out of the house.

The finals of the US Open Tennis Championships at Forest Hills was on TV, and I figured I would watch it when I got home since I had nothing better to do.

I made no effort with my appearance because I was as sick as a dog and who was going to see me besides my family? Or so I thought.

My hair was dirty and pulled back into a greasy bun. I wore overalls and sneakers. I looked like walking death.

When my sister and I returned home there was an unknown car in front of my house, and I asked her whose it was. She told me that it belonged to our brother's friend, Tommy. "They work and play tennis together."

Up until now I would have known every single person that one of my four siblings was friends with, but having spent the last two summers on the West Coast, this one had slipped by me.

I was curious. I walked into our den. There, in his tennis whites and a tan body, was my brother's friend. He made a quick introduction, I said hello, and I quickly turned on my heels and went upstairs, mortified by my appearance. Since when did my older brother have a cute friend? Never.

I proceeded to watch the US Open in my room and rest, vowing not to reappear until that gorgeous boy was gone. I must have fallen asleep because I woke up to my mother calling to me that it was time to eat.

For the moment, I had forgotten the incident. It was a Sunday, so all seven of us ate dinner together in the dining room as we did every week.

When I came downstairs and walked into the dining room, there was Tommy, sitting at the table along with the rest of my family. I thought I would pass out.

I sat at the table with my head in my hand and never said a word. He charmed my parents and ate everything my mother made, much to her delight. As soon as dinner was over, I excused myself, mortified for the second time that day.

About two months later, when I was starting to feel like myself again, my brother asked me if I would be interested in a double date.

"With whom?" I asked.

"Remember my friend, Tommy?"

"Oh yeah, the tennis player, right?" I was trying to play it cool but inside I was bursting.

He explained to me that he liked a girl a lot, but she was playing hard to get. He thought if his friend and I went on a double date with them, it would help him out.

What he didn't tell me was that Tommy had inquired about me several times after that fateful dinner in my dining room. So we each thought we were going out with my brother and potential girlfriend to do him a favor.

That night led to a full-blown relationship. We fell in love, and two years later he proposed. I accepted on one condition—that we live in California. It wasn't a hard sell, and a year later we were married and heading out to Los Angeles. That was forty years ago!

More times than not, I've learned that life's drawbacks can yield lucky consequences. If I hadn't gotten sick, who knows where my life would have led?

49

FROM THE DARKNESS COMES THE LIGHT
Michelle & Mark

AFTER THIRTY YEARS OF MARRIAGE, I could no longer live in a lonely loveless marriage.

It was a hard decision but necessary for my serenity. My heart hurt but I had to move on.

Although I often felt like a failure, I came out of the marriage with three amazing children and my independence as a successful business owner.

After struggling through a year of separation I felt like I was finally set free, and it felt great!

I was enjoying my alone time and took my time to heal.

Soon after, I was at holiday dinner with friends and family. A few were eager to set me up, but I easily turned them all down.

However, life totally changed one night when I was with a dear friend and her husband. They were both so excited when they told me that they had the perfect guy for me.

I agreed to this one. Why? Was I really ready or was fate stepping in? Why had I turned down every one else?

I got my answer over sushi on our first dinner. We had an instant connection. It felt so right.

With Mark I was totally myself. We connected in every way. We have the same family values, we both started our own businesses, we love golf, biking, games, travel, just being together and enjoying each other's company.

After so much loneliness and disappointment, I feel I met my soul mate. We respect and value each other.

His love repaired my heart and showed me what love was all about.

We dated for five years when he surprised me and proposed at 6:30 in the morning on a Sunday bike ride.

We've been married for three years and have melded our families beautifully. Our homes are always very busy and our lives are complete

I am so grateful, that every single day I write him a thank you note!

We both look ahead to our life together to creating new memories.

It's so true that from the darkness, one can see the light!

A very wise person once said this to me. "The rear-view mirror of a car is very small that represents the past. The windshield in the front is wide, large and open. That is the present and the future. What do you want to focus on?"

I left my past behind, and I look forward to living in the present having new adventures together. You can too!

Leave your past behind and keep your heart opened to what may be ahead.

SHE SAID, HE SAID
Linda & Ron

LINDA SAID...

I became a widow at the age of sixty-two after being happily married for over four decades. I could not think of dating until a year later, when my children insisted it was time.

Frankly, I never thought I would have any difficulty meeting a nice man.

The first time I was asked out on a date came from a much older man in my community. Though I refused him many times he would send me lovely notes, the last being a poem by Omar Khayyam. I was intrigued and accepted his date.

Although he was a man of intelligence and influence as well as a philanthropist, it was not enough to hold onto that relationship. The age gap was just too big.

I then had to take matters into my own hands and began my search for a man of good standing. JDate and Match were to be my go-to places on the advice offered by my children and friends.

On the dating sites, I was obsessive about who these too-perfect strangers were and investigated anyone who contacted me.

I had heard quite a few frightening stories about these sites and was determined not to be careless. I never gave my name or phone number to anyone before I checked them out on the internet.

Apart from those in whom I had no interest, I eliminated anyone who was not prepared to give me his name without knowing mine. After googling the possibilities, and without going into detail, suffice it to say that the men did not check out well.

I had reluctantly come to realize that the dating business, at least for me, was bankrupt.

I was reconciled to live out the rest of my days alone when out of the blue, a friend of mine told me about a very nice recent widower at our club. She would introduce me to him the following week at our weekly film that he too attended.

She pointed him out to me, and I was surprised that I had not seen him before. He was a tall, dark, and handsome attorney.

When the film ended, my friend and I made our way out of the room, making sure we bumped into him. She said hello to him, but neglected to introduce us, and we all followed to the restaurant we favored. We walked and walked and walked some more, the five of us in a row with my friend and this man chatting away. Still no introduction.

Just a minute before we reached the restaurant entrance, I introduced myself by interrupting them. She never said anything about the meeting, and I said nothing to her.

The following week, he was again at the film screening with another couple who were new acquaintances of mine. Without thinking, I got up from my usual table of friends including the friend who never made the introduction and headed to theirs.

I used an excuse for stopping by and he stood up, which I thought was very gallant and impressive. My stated reason for the visit was that I was a very active patron of a film festival in our city, and I was asking if they would be interested.

He immediately said he was, so I handed out brochures to each of them. He then asked me for my phone number for any questions he might have.

I was immediately taken with him.

The next morning, I did something that I had never done before. I called my new friend who was with him the night before and asked her if she thought it would be okay to call him, as he was still a recent widower.

Was I perhaps being too aggressive, much like the brisket brigade Joan Rivers used to joke about?

She said, "Go for it," and gave me his number.

Gathering up my courage, I called Ron and reminded him who I was and was glad he remembered.

While not quite sure how to phrase it, I told him I too was widowed and asked if he would like a new friend. He immediately said that he would and asked if he could call me in a bit. True to his word, he did, and we made our first date.

On the way to the restaurant, I felt lightheaded and slipped. I took his arm, comfortably telling him of my sometimes low blood pressure when I stand up too quickly.

He still likes to reminisce about that moment as he felt so comfortable holding me as well.

We're still holding on to each other. It is a month short of three years together.

When COVID struck, we decided that I would move into his place as it was larger than mine.

Strange how that international calamity brought us fully together.

We have not been separated since, and we just moved into a new condo that we love a few months ago.

I am a very fortunate woman to have found love, not through dating sites, bars, or introductions by friends or family but by an inner pull that we both had. And I'm so glad I took that first bold step, from which I never turned back. We are most definitely meant to be.

Ron said...

My partner of three-plus years and I were both widowed when we met; in my own case, quite recently.

I had been married for almost fifty-four years to a woman whom I had met when we were both teenagers and lost her quite suddenly.

Sadly, for reasons unrelated to the fast-growing cancer that came out of nowhere to take her life, I had been playing the role of caregiver for the past few years.

When she passed, I found myself both bereft and alone. In Boca Raton, Florida, where people losing spouses is sadly all too common, men who suddenly become single quickly find themselves the focus of much attention. Even for men like me in their mid-seventies, the joke is that all you need to be eligible is a pulse. My pulse was still functioning, if not pounding.

I was more than a little surprised at the onslaught of unsolicited tuna casseroles, which I would not eat, short of starvation, and chocolate chip cookies, which I devoured with abandon.

Into this scenario of love amidst the ruins came the fetching woman with whom I now share my life.

In our case, how we connected was a combination of karma, or its Jewish relative, B'shert, and careful planning—more on her part than mine.

I had just been to a late afternoon weekly Sunday foreign film with a couple who had been close friends with me and my late wife, and we were having drinks at our club. My now partner, who was actively involved with a local film festival, came over to our table, ostensibly to see if the other couple was interested in subscribing to her film festival.

When she approached the table, I, being old school, rose from my seat, taken by her stunning appearance. I was tempted to ask her to join us for dinner, but I knew she had been sitting with another group of people and I didn't want my request to be turned down.

She provided us all with information about the film festival, which conveniently included her phone number. We went on to have a nice dinner, albeit without her.

The next morning, as I was about to leave my apartment for a tennis game, the phone rang. It was her, and she began by reminding me that we had met the night before—not that I needed any reminding, as I had been quite taken with her. She said that she had never made such a phone call before but understood that like her, I was widowed, and wanted to know if I was interested in having a friend.

More than a friend, I thought, but told her I would like that very much, but was on my way out the door for tennis and said I would call her back later. After my match, I called and asked her out for the following Friday. Happily, as the old saying goes, the rest was history.

As for the karma factor, it clearly played a role in that I just happened to be with a couple that evening whom she knew, and the film festival of which she was a patron provided a pretext for her coming over to our table. Unbeknownst to me at the time, I was the sole reason for the visit and the film festival pitch was merely part of the subterfuge.

This only goes to prove that no cultural endeavor, however contrived, is ever truly in vain. If I hadn't gone to the movies that afternoon and followed it up by going to the restaurant, which provided bargain drinks and food for film attendees, we mightn't have met.

As for the planning, all credit goes to her. Her friend with whom she had been sitting had failed to introduce us, and she wisely took matters into her own hands, and I've been all the luckier for it.

And now, a few weeks shy of three years later, we have given up our separate Florida condos and are living together in a wonderful new place that is home for us. Oh yeah, that pulse I referred to up above pounds anew.

Encouraging Words of Hope

THE RECURRING THEME IN ALL of these wonderful stories of how couples met and fell in love is, "It can happen to you." Hence, the title of the book. Throughout the stories you will find advice from people just like you who had given up hope of finding or found love out of the blue. Here are some of their nuggets of wisdom:

"Let everyone you know that you are looking for love. You never know when it will find you!"

"Never ever give up. Love happens when you least expect it."

"Trust the universe. Stay in the present and please don't quit before the miracle.

"Do not settle. Where there's life, there is hope! Remember, you only need one!"

"Find things that bring you personal joy. Be open to new people and experiences. Never, ever stop believing that he/she is out there. Let the universe bring you both together."

"Be true to yourself. Keep growing, loving yourself and keep open to possibilities."

"Never throw in the towel. Love is everywhere, even on those days when we can't seem to see."

"Take risks, get out of your comfort zone, don't be controlled by your negative inner voice telling you it's not going to happen for you."

"Make it a great life with or without a relationship and trust that love will happen when it's supposed to."

"Keep your heart open on every level. Expand your dating pool, work on your inner core, tell your truth. And remember that it only takes one special person."

"Always stay open to possibilities and give the person you thought was not your type a chance. At the end of the day, all you need is love!"

"Let life take its course. Be happy right where you are and remain open to serendipitous meetings!"

"Fill your head with positive thoughts. Just because there's no love interest when you wake up tomorrow doesn't mean there won't be an unexpected meeting by the evening."

"Keep your mind and heart open to all possibilities, whether or not they fit the photos in your head. Having a checklist keeps you lonely."

"I first had to find love in me, before I could accept that someone else could love me."

"After experiencing the emotional trauma of a fractured love affair, you will most probably want to cocoon and protect yourself from any more hurt. While that is necessary for personal healing, it is most important to remain positive about yourself."

"We think we can control our future, but we can't. The best we can do is enjoy the moments that we are given. Make the very best of them."

"Even in the bleakest moments, hold on tight to your dreams with hope and an open heart."

"Love the life you live. Even if it's over when you turn one hundred, it will be over way too soon."

"Be willing to enjoy the relationships that come with dating for what they are and walk away when it no longer serves you."

"We never really know where a love connection can pop up."

"Don't quit before the miracle. Keep believing in yourself and the universe to bring you love when it's time."

"Even if you go shopping for bananas, always keep your heart and eyes open. You may wind up with a fabulous person in your life!"

"There are happy endings and new beginnings if you can see beyond the obstacles."

"Don't ever give up finding your diamond. Keep your heart open until you find someone whose imperfections are perfect for you!"

"Life is a mysterious adventure filled with the unexpected. Don't give up your dreams. And remember that *fate* has many disguises and has a habit of finding you when least expected."

"Fall in love with someone who is your best friend whom you can have fun with doing absolutely anything and nothing. One who supports you and loves you for you!"

"Create the very best life you can. Learn everything you can about yourself. Keep growing so that when a serendipitous encounter happens you are prepared and ready to love and be loved. Even when you had very powerfully said never again!"

"I guess finding love is like chasing a butterfly in an open field. If we try too hard to catch it, it evades us. However, when we are at peace with ourselves, the butterfly will land on our shoulders when we least expect it."

Acknowledgements

It is said that it takes a village to raise a child. I say, it takes a team of enthusiastic cheerleaders to write a book. I'm so grateful for all of mine.

MY STORY CONTRIBUTORS. There wouldn't be a book (even with a team of the best cheerleaders) without the fifty outstanding women and men who generously shared their intimate and authentic stories with me. We are collectively making a difference in the lives of our readers. I love and appreciate each one of you.

MY MOTHER HARRIET RIPP, the creator of the term unconditional love. If you were alive today, you would be shamelessly selling this book on the street corners and beauty parlors in Pelham Parkway, Bronx. I was blessed to have you as my mother. You instilled the confidence in me to write this book.

MY FATHER, SAMUEL RIPP. You gave me two life lessons at age nine that have remained with me and helped shape me. First, never say woulda, coulda, or shoulda. You were ahead of your time. A book of the same name came out years later. I listened. Second, an intelligent person is never bored because of books.

My daughter, Sloane Seiler Feldman. Thank you for taking me seriously on this project, especially after listening to all my "great ideas" throughout your life. I knew you really heard me this time when you posted my vision on Facebook. I hope you are as proud of me as I am of you. I love you, Sloaney Baloney.

Susan Brettschneider, the only other member of the Best-Friend Cousin's Club. I saved your life swimming when we were nine and ten and you have repaid me with your unconditional lifelong love! There is nothing that you don't know about me and yet you always have my back. Thank you for your unwavering support, always!

Denise Richardson. It all began with your encouragement over our very long lunch at the end of September, when we shared our future dreams. I wrote the date of October 3, 2021, on a paper napkin and committed myself to beginning this project. Who is more shocked, you or me, that I actually completed it? All you had to do was say it was a great idea and I ran with it. Thank you, my dear friend. Looking forward to our next Jersey Boys outing. Is it number thirteen or fourteen?

Claire Bukzin-Hakim. Your enthusiasm and immediate belief in my idea for this book made me soar and inspired me to complete this project. I'm so grateful for your support of my vision, for your love, and for your generosity of spirit. You are a fantastic person and friend.

Stephanie Krobot, my head cheerleader. My Martha Stewart, Marie Kondo, and Emily Post all rolled into one fabulous person. It was love at first sight when we worked together at New Woman Magazine. Our thought-provoking conversations always inspire me. Your love and generosity are an incredible gift to me. My gratitude runs deep!

Laura Gabriel. After all these years I am still in awe of your deep commitment to the truth, to personal growth, to service, to making a difference, and to loving me. Wherever we are, wherever we go, the car, the lakes, the diners, etc., you are always open to intimate conversations that have peals of laughter thrown in. It's been an awesome ride together and it's not over. I'm forever grateful for our friendship and your support and ideas for this project.

JILL ROMAN. My beautiful (inside and outside) forever friend, my fashion and artistic director. We didn't grow up together, but we grew up together. From giggles, secrets, and boy talks, to spirituality and personal growth, we've covered it all. I love our friendship more than you know.

JOY WESTON. You are a trailblazer as an author, which inspired me to put my pen to paper too, following in your footsteps. I can always call upon you to give me your fascinating Joy-isms.

LAURA SLUTSKY, for texting me almost every day with new book title ideas and couples for me to interview. Your talents are boundless, and I look forward to seeing your screenplay at the AMC one of these days.

CHARLES FAVREAU. Thank you for your support, which I have counted on for over fifty years, beginning with our game board idea, Sidhartha, The Game of Life. Why didn't we make that a reality? Maybe that will be the next project for us. I'm in if you are. We have always been cheerleaders for each other's ideas. It will never be any other way.

SHEILA TRONN for always being willing to help in any way. I always appreciate your creative ideas for this book, which seem to flow out of you so effortlessly. You are a supportive and loving friend.

ELLIE KING. Another love at first sight friend. We met on a double date in the late '70s, and never saw the guys again. Bonus, we became the best of friends. Ellie, you were born to be a cheerleader for all. You have that innate quality to make everyone feel that they are the most important person on the planet, and you express it with enthusiasm. That's how I feel when I'm lucky enough to be in your company. I can hear you loudly cheering for me in the stands.

KATE GRANADO. A very special shout-out. My trusted confidant; sage, tireless, creative, wise woman. What would I have done without you? It's a good thing that I didn't have to pay for the long-distance phone conversations with you in Ecuador. The bill would have been tremendous. Our ability to laugh together through it all kept me sane through this process. I owe you big-time for all the red pencils you used for all the pre-editing that you did. You are a brilliant writer and an incredible friend. Always a yes to me with a smile. I love you from the top and bottom of my heart. As always, a special thank you to Ira Garey for making you Seventeen Magazine's West Coast rep, or we'd never have met.

ARTHUR GRANADO. Thank you for letting me borrow your amazing wife for six weeks. And thank you for not rolling your eyes whenever I called, or did you?

TO MY PUBLISHER, CHERYL BENTON, The Three Tomatoes Publishing. How lucky was I to have found you? Thank you for being such an enthusiastic yes during our very first conversation. Each time I submitted my stories and you responded positively, it kept me motivated, excited, and confident to carry on. You are a pleasure to work with, so easygoing and very knowledgeable. I'm deeply grateful for you taking me on as a client and making my dream a reality.

ABOUT THE AUTHOR

AN INCURABLE ROMANTIC, NANCY RIPP WHITE has been collecting stories of how couples met for years. She would sometimes share those stories with her female friends who were disillusioned with dating, especially online dating, and bemoaning that there are no good men left. Her stories gave them hope.

Nancy herself has been married and divorced. She's been a dater, and a single mom. She's kissed her share of frogs and princes. She's broken a few hearts and had her heart broken. She's gone through the throes of love, loss, and remorse and she's had many joyful, fulfilling loves.

Navigating through her own personal challenges, she discovered a life-changing truth—the importance of self-worth, self-trust, self-confidence, and self-love, which lead to feeling empowered and becoming ready when love appears. Motivated to help other women, she became a certified life coach specializing in relationships. For over two decades she has successfully counseled hundreds of women on the life-changing power of self-worth and self-love.

She is committed to teaching, cheerleading, and supporting women to let their light and inner beauty shine to create the lives they had only wished for. It can happen to you.

If you are interested in finding out more about Nancy's coaching practice, or if you have a love connection story to share, you can reach her via email at lovelifeu@aol.com.

Made in the USA
Middletown, DE
26 January 2022

59756352R00108